Towards Green Growth

OECD

This work is published on the responsibility of the Secretary-General of the OECD. The opinions expressed and arguments employed herein do not necessarily reflect the official views of the Organisation or of the governments of its member countries.

Please cite this publication as:
OECD (2011), *Towards Green Growth*, OECD Publishing.
http://dx.doi.org/10.1787/9789264111318-en

ISBN 978-92-64-09497-0 (print)
ISBN 978-92-64-11131-8 (PDF)

The statistical data for Israel are supplied by and under the responsibility of the relevant Israeli authorities. The use of such data by the OECD is without prejudice to the status of the Golan Heights, East Jerusalem and Israeli settlements in the West Bank under the terms of international law.

Cover design by advitam for the OECD.

Corrigenda to OECD publications may be found on line at: *www.oecd.org/publishing/corrigenda*.

Introduction by the Secretary-General

The OECD Green Growth Strategy: A lens for examining growth

The world economy is slowly, and unevenly, coming out of the worst crisis most of us have ever known. While dealing with immediate problems such as high unemployment, inflationary pressures or fiscal deficits, we have to look to the future and devise new ways of ensuring that the growth and progress we have come to take for granted are assured in the years to come.

A return to "business as usual" would indeed be unwise and ultimately unsustainable, involving risks that could impose human costs and constraints on economic growth and development. It could result in increased water scarcity, resource bottlenecks, air and water pollution, climate change and biodiversity loss which would be irreversible.

Strategies to achieve greener growth are needed. If we want to make sure that the progress in living standards we have seen these past fifty years does not grind to a halt, we have to find new ways of producing and consuming things. And even redefine what we mean by progress and how we measure it. And we have to make sure to take our citizens with us on this journey, in particular to prepare the people with the right skills to reap the employment benefits from the structural change.

But we cannot just start from scratch. Changing current patterns of growth, consumer habits, technology, and infrastructure is a long-term project, and we will have to live with the consequences of past decisions for a long time. This "path dependency" is likely to intensify systemic environmental risks even if we were to get policy settings right relatively swiftly.

The modern economy was created thanks to innovation and thrives on it, and in turn the economy encourages new ways of doing things and the invention of new products. That will continue to be the case. Non-technological changes and innovation such as new business models, work patterns, city planning or transportation arrangements will also be instrumental in driving green growth.

No government has all the technological, scientific, financial and other resources needed to implement green growth alone. The challenges are global, and recently we have seen encouraging international efforts to tackle environmental issues collectively, including the path-breaking Cancun agreements to address climate change.

At the OECD Ministerial Council Meeting in June 2009, Ministers acknowledged that green and growth can go hand-in-hand, and asked the OECD to develop a Green Growth Strategy. Since then, we have been working with a wide range of partners from across government and civil society to provide a framework for how countries can achieve economic growth and development while at the same time combating climate change and preventing costly environmental degradation and the inefficient use of natural resources.

This publication summarises the work done so far. As a lens through which to examine growth, the analysis presented here is an important first step to designing green growth strategies while at the same time providing an actionable policy framework for policy makers in advanced, emerging and developing economies.

The OECD will continue to support global efforts to promote green growth, especially in view of the Rio+20 Conference. The next step will see green growth reflected in OECD country reviews and the output of future OECD work on green growth indicators, toolkits and sectoral studies, to support countries' implementation efforts towards green growth.

We have set ourselves ambitious targets, but I am confident that by working together we will reach them.

Angel Gurría
OECD Secretary-General

Table of contents

Tables

Figures

Boxes

Executive summary

Green growth means fostering economic growth and development while ensuring that natural assets continue to provide the resources and environmental services on which our well-being relies. To do this it must catalyse investment and innovation which will underpin sustained growth and give rise to new economic opportunities.

A return to "business as usual" would be unwise and ultimately unsustainable, involving risks that could impose human costs and constraints on economic growth and development. It could result in increased water scarcity, resource bottlenecks, air and water pollution, climate change and biodiversity loss which would be irreversible; thus the need for strategies to achieve greener growth.

Sources of green growth

Green growth has the potential to address economic and environmental challenges and open up new sources of growth through the following channels:

- **Productivity.** Incentives for greater efficiency in the use of resources and natural assets: enhancing productivity, reducing waste and energy consumption and making resources available to highest value use.

- **Innovation.** Opportunities for innovation, spurred by policies and framework conditions that allow for new ways of addressing environmental problems.

- **New markets.** Creation of new markets by stimulating demand for green technologies, goods, and services; creating potential for new job opportunities.

- **Confidence.** Boosting investor confidence through greater predictability and stability around how governments are going to deal with major environmental issues.

- **Stability.** More balanced macroeconomic conditions, reduced resource price volatility and supporting fiscal consolidation through, for instance, reviewing the composition and efficiency of public spending and increasing revenues through the pricing of pollution.

It can also reduce risks of negative shocks to growth from:

- **Resource bottlenecks** which make investment more costly, such as the need for capital-intensive infrastructure when water supplies become scarce or their quality decreases (*e.g.* desalinisation equipment). In this regard, the loss of natural capital can exceed the gains generated by economic activity, undermining the ability to sustain future growth.

- **Imbalances** in natural systems which raise the risk of more profound, abrupt, highly damaging, and potentially irreversible, effects – as has happened to some fish stocks and as could happen with damage to biodiversity under unabated climate change. Attempts to identify potential thresholds suggest that in some cases – climate change, global nitrogen cycles and biodiversity loss – these have already been exceeded.

A framework for green growth

There is no "one-size-fits-all" prescription for implementing strategies for green growth. Greening the growth path of an economy depends on policy and institutional settings, level of development, resource endowments and particular environmental pressure points. Advanced, emerging, and developing countries will face different challenges and opportunities, as will countries with differing economic and political circumstances.

There are, on the other hand, common considerations that need to be addressed in all settings. Most importantly, good economic policy lies at the heart of any strategy for green growth. A flexible, dynamic economy is likely to be best for growth and to enable the transition to a greener growth path. Greening growth will require much more efficient use of resources to minimise environmental pressures. Efficient resource use and management is a core goal of economic policy and many fiscal and regulatory interventions that are not normally associated with a "green" agenda will be involved. And in every case, policy action requires looking across a very wide range of policies, not just traditionally "green" policies.

A green growth strategy is centred on mutually reinforcing aspects of economic and environmental policy. It takes into account the full value of natural capital as a factor of production and its role in growth. It focuses on cost-effective ways of attenuating environmental pressures to effect a transition towards new patterns of growth that will avoid crossing critical local, regional and global environmental thresholds.

Innovation will play a key role. Existing production technology and consumer behaviour can only be expected to produce positive outcomes up to a point; a frontier, beyond which depleting natural capital has negative consequences for overall growth. We do not know precisely where this frontier lies in all cases but we do know that the ability of reproducible capital to substitute for (depleted) natural capital is limited in the absence of innovation. By pushing the frontier outward, innovation can help to decouple growth from natural capital depletion.

A green growth strategy also recognises that focusing on GDP as a measure of economic progress overlooks the contribution of natural assets to wealth, health and well-being. It therefore targets a range of measures of progress, encompassing the quality and composition of growth, and how this affects people's wealth and welfare. In this and many other respects, green growth is an essential component of sustainable development (Box 0.1).

The economic costs arising from the emission of some pollutants and the over-exploitation of some resources are relatively well-known. Clear benefits will arise once the right policies are implemented. In some cases, the size and timing of payoffs from maintaining ecosystem services – the benefits humans derive from nature – are subject to uncertainty because interactions between ecosystem services, climate change and biodiversity are complex. Nonetheless, action taken now to insure against unfavourable, irreversible or even catastrophic outcomes can avoid significant economic costs in the future.

Economic policy decisions need to incorporate a longer time horizon. Patterns of growth and technological change build on one another creating path dependency and technological and institutional lock in. Environmental impacts are also cumulative and sometimes irreversible. These create strong links between decisions today and economic opportunities in the future.

Box 0.1.   Green growth and sustainable development

Sustainable development provides an important context for green growth. The OECD Green Growth Strategy leverages off the substantial body of analysis and policy effort that flowed from the 1992 Rio Earth Summit. It develops a clear and focused agenda for delivering on a number of Rio's key aspirations.

Green growth has not been conceived as not a replacement for sustainable development, but rather should be considered a subset of it. It is narrower in scope, entailing an operational policy agenda that can help achieve concrete, measurable progress at the interface between the economy and the environment. It provides a strong focus on fostering the necessary conditions for innovation, investment and competition that can give rise to new sources of economic growth – consistent with resilient ecosystems.

Green growth strategies need to pay specific attention to many of the social issues and equity concerns that can arise as a direct result of greening the economy – both at the national and international level. This is essential for successful implementation of green growth policies. Strategies should be implemented in parallel with initiatives centering on the broader social pillar of sustainable development.

The Strategy develops an actionable policy framework that is designed to be flexible enough to be tailored to differing national circumstances and stages of development. In partnership with initiatives by other international organisations, including UNEP, UNESCAP and the World Bank, OECD green growth work has been planned to contribute to the objectives of Rio+20.

Matching green growth policies and poverty reduction objectives will be important for adapting this framework to emerging and developing countries. There are important complementarities between green growth and poverty reduction, which can be capitalised to help drive progress towards the Millennium Development Goals. These include, for example, bringing more efficient infrastructure to people (*e.g.* in water and transport), alleviating poor health associated with environmental degradation and introducing efficient technologies that can reduce costs and increase productivity, while easing environmental pressure. Given the centrality of natural assets in low-income countries, green growth policies can reduce vulnerability to environmental risks and increase the livelihood security of the poor.

The essentials of green growth strategies

Green growth strategies need to encourage greener behaviour by firms and consumers, facilitate smooth and just reallocation of jobs, capital and technology towards greener activities and provide adequate incentives and support to green innovation. Misguided government policies, market constraints and distortions all lead to or arise from market failures, which mean there is often a gap between private returns from economic activity and the overall benefits that accrue to society. Green growth policies aim to close that gap and raise returns to "green" investment and innovation. They also aim to minimise the distributional consequences of change for the least advantaged groups of society and manage any negative economic impacts on firms while retaining incentives for improved economic performance.

Implementing a green growth strategy will involve a mix of instruments which draw from two broad sets of policies. The first set includes framework conditions that mutually reinforce economic growth and the conservation of natural capital. Included in this are core fiscal and regulatory settings, such as tax and competition policy, which, if well designed and executed, maximise the efficient allocation of resources. This is the familiar agenda of economic policy with the added realisation that it can be as good for the environment as for the economy. To these settings should be added innovation policies[1] that place a premium on the inventiveness that is needed if we are to use natural capital much more sparingly and efficiently.

The second set encompasses policies targeted at incentivising efficient use of natural resources and making pollution more expensive. They include a mix of price-based and other policy instruments. The stand-alone annex *Tools for Delivering on Green Growth* details the broad policy toolkit for green growth that these two sets embrace.

While national circumstances will differ, putting a price on pollution or on the over-exploitation of scarce natural resources – through mechanisms such as taxes or tradable permit systems – should be a central element of the policy mix. Pricing mechanisms tend to minimise the costs of achieving a given objective and provide incentives for further efficiency gains and innovation. Importantly, increased use of environmentally related taxes can play a role in growth-oriented tax reform; by helping to shifting (part of) the tax burden away from more distortive corporate and personal income taxes and social contributions. Taxes on energy and CO_2 can also be a natural part of a wider fiscal consolidation package, offering an attractive alternative to higher taxes on labour or business income or deep cuts in public expenditure.

Not every situation lends itself to market instruments. In certain cases, well-designed regulation, active technology-support policies and voluntary approaches may be more appropriate or an important complement to market instruments. In addition, the responsiveness of businesses and consumers to price signals can, in many situations, be strengthened through information-based measures that highlight the consequences of environmental damage caused by specific activities and the availability of cleaner alternatives.

Changing the payoffs in the economy is only part of the solution. Societies become dependent on institutions and technologies with which they are familiar. Social and economic inertia can be so strong that even quite large changes in pay-offs will not change behaviour. A strong capability to innovate is essential to establish the capacity for breakthroughs and new patterns of production and consumption. Innovation can generate new sources of growth that better reflect the full value of natural capital to society and reduce the cost of addressing environmental risks. Green growth strategies need to address the following challenges for green innovation:

- Many environmental externalities are under-priced or not priced at all. The consequences of such externalities may not be well understood. For example, a carbon price can help to incentivise innovation to tackle climate change, but current levels of carbon prices are low, leaving a considerable gap.

- Path dependency and dominance of existing technologies and systems can make it very difficult for some new technologies to compete, establish a place in the market and scale up, which is why temporary support may be needed in certain cases. Innovation support instruments must be carefully designed to foster the emergence and uptake of efficient technologies while minimising the risk of technology lock-in, lack of competition or crowding out of private investment.

- Barriers to trade and investment can place a serious break on the development and diffusion of green technologies globally. Reducing these barriers while providing effective protection and enforcement of intellectual property rights (IPRs) are essential to encourage the development and diffusion of technologies and the facilitation of foreign direct investment and licensing.

Greening growth will also require policies to establish network infrastructure which is suitable for next generation technologies, especially in areas such as energy, water, transport and communications networks. Green infrastructure investments can help avoid costly lock-in of inefficient patterns of growth. They can lift economic growth and bring social and health benefits. In developing economies, there will be opportunities for leap-frogging to new forms of infrastructure development. Leveraging public and private financing – *e.g.* through public-private partnerships, a mixture of tariffs and taxes, facilitating investment by major institutional partners through reforming regulatory barriers and sound long-term policy signals, and development assistance – will be necessary given the large-scale investments required in most countries.

Ultimately, what matters for the success of a green growth strategy is a well-defined framework for action and a consistent set of economic and environmental policy criteria. It will need to build on a high degree of co-ordination among ministries and levels of government as well as stakeholders outside government, to identify a policy mix suitable to local conditions. In many cases, developing appropriate institutional capacity will be an essential condition for integrating green growth into core economic strategies and other government policies, and for ensuring a leading role for finance, economic and environment agencies.

Ensuring a smooth labour market transition

Greener growth will see new jobs created, including skilled jobs in emerging green innovative activities. But some jobs will be at risk so there is a need to facilitate the re-allocation of workers from contracting to expanding sectors, such as those that replace polluting activities with cleaner alternatives or provide environmental services.

Labour market policies should focus on preserving employment, not jobs. They need to ensure that workers and firms are able to adjust quickly to changes brought about by the greening of the economy, including by seizing new opportunities. By helping workers to move from jobs in contracting sectors to jobs in expanding sectors, they can also help to assure a just sharing of adjustment costs occasioned by the transition.[2] New skills will be needed and this will require appropriate education policies. While many existing skills will remain appropriate, skill mismatches and gaps may emerge. Training and re-training programmes will be a key component of labour market policies.

The scale of adjustment should not be overstated. For example, significant reductions of greenhouse gas emissions can be achieved with only limited effects on the pace of employment growth. Indeed labour market performance can improve if revenues from carbon pricing are used to promote labour demand. Furthermore, this does not take into account the positive impact on employment as a result of strategies fostering sources of green growth.

Addressing distributional aspects

Accounting for the distributional impacts of greening growth will be crucial for its public acceptability. There is a widespread perception that the distributional effects of some policy instruments will inevitably be regressive. This is not necessarily the case, but unless these concerns are addressed the acceptability of some key policies may be called into question.

For example, the phasing out of fossil fuel subsidies will have positive impacts on the environment and the economy in the aggregate but may entail adverse consequences for some nations or population groups in the short-term. The loss caused by higher fuel prices will be immediately obvious and significant for some, but the economic, social and environmental gains will take longer to materialise and be more diffuse. Targeted compensatory measures will need to be introduced, particularly in emerging markets where some populations are most vulnerable to transitional costs associated with greening growth.

International co-operation for green growth

Creating a global architecture that is conducive to green growth will require enhanced international co-operation. Strengthening arrangements for managing global public goods, especially in biodiversity and climate, hold the key to addressing co-ordination and incentive problems. The agreements reached at

Cancun on climate change give reason to be optimistic that progress can be made but ongoing efforts are needed. Financial flows in particular need to become both an engine for growth and development as well as an incentive to maintain the quality of the global commons.

Official Development Assistance (ODA) can continue to play an important role to create enabling conditions for green growth, targeting areas where incentives for private investment are limited and flows are scarce, including essential infrastructure and human and institutional capacity building. Increased co-operation in science and technology will need to be underscored by more concerted approaches to accelerate technology development and diffusion and build research capacity in developing countries.

Increased efforts to boost global trade and investment flows could help underpin sustained growth and diffusion of green technologies. There is also a need to ensure that the development prospects of low-income countries are not undermined through the potential spill-over effects of domestic trade and investment measures. Some countries have expressed concern that trade and investment could be affected if the green growth policy agenda were captured by protectionist interests.

While investment protectionism associated with green growth policies has not been found to be a major problem to date, continued vigilance should be encouraged. The OECD-hosted Freedom of Investment Roundtable will continue to monitor investment measures to ensure that they are not used as disguised protectionism. Its recent communication on "Harnessing Freedom of Investment for Green Growth" aiming at making governments' environmental and investment policy goals mutually supportive is reproduced in Annex 1.

Monitoring progress towards green growth

Monitoring progress towards green growth should draw on groups of indicators which describe and track changes in: *(i)* productivity in the use of environmental assets and natural resources; *(ii)* the natural asset base; *(iii)* the environmental dimensions of quality of life; *(iv)* policy responses and economic opportunities. For each of these groups, a list of indicators has been proposed in a companion report *Towards Green Growth - Monitoring Progress: OECD Indicators*. This is work in progress and will be further elaborated as data become available and as concepts evolve.

Work to date suggests that environmental and resource productivity has been rising. While there are significant differences between countries, growth of GDP and other measures of output tend to outstrip growth of environmental inputs into the production system. However, improved environmental productivity has not been accompanied by absolute decreases in environmental pressure or the sustainable use of some natural assets.

Indicators that measure the "green economy" need to be interpreted carefully. Judged simply by the size of industries involved in the production of environmental goods and services, today's "green economy" is relatively small. However, economic opportunities, entrepreneurship and innovation in conjunction with green growth can arise in all sectors so an assessment based on green industries understates the economic importance of environmentally related activities.

Green Growth Strategy: Next steps

To succeed, national green growth strategies will need to be mainstreamed into government policies. The OECD can contribute to this in a number of ways. The framework and policy insights of this report can be tailored to account for country-specific circumstances, and provide guidance for continued analysis in the form of country reviews. Such work can offer opportunities for an in-depth appraisal of the way in which policies are working together (or not) to drive greener growth. The development and refinement of the green growth toolkits that will accompany this Strategy can further support policy implementation at the national level.

Experience gained through both country reviews and general policy assessment could lead to the development of an analytical tool that would identify country-specific policy priorities on the basis of a cross-country analysis and understanding of what is good practice. This would benefit from continued work on green growth indicators and measurement issues. Indeed, an important measurement agenda arises from confronting indicators with available and internationally comparable data. The OECD will be advancing the measurement agenda in the years ahead so as to improve the possibilities for tracking the transition to green growth in OECD and other economies.

Further analytical work on the costs and benefits of various policy instruments also needs to be carried out. Moreover, work on issue-specific and sector-specific studies will yield more concrete insights into the implications of greening growth in a number of areas. Early priorities include food and agriculture, the energy sector, water, biodiversity and development co-operation, as well as policies governing cities and rural area development.

Finally, future OECD work on green growth will be based on a deepened collaboration with other international organisations, including UN agencies, the World Bank and the Global Green Growth Institute, as well as a range of stakeholders, to facilitate the exchange of experience and best practices, and to help promote international arrangements that are conducive to greener growth in both developed and developing countries.

Notes

1   These include sound innovation policies elaborated in the *OECD Innovation Strategy*.

2   Lessons from the *OECD Reassessed Job Strategy* can be useful to that effect.

Chapter 1. The need for green growth strategies

The world faces twin challenges: expanding economic opportunities for a growing global population, and addressing environmental pressures that, if left unaddressed, could undermine our ability to seize these opportunities.

Green growth strategies are needed because:

- *The impacts of economic activity on environmental systems are creating imbalances which are putting economic growth and development at risk. Increased efforts to address climate change and biodiversity loss are needed to address these risks.*

- *Natural capital, encompassing natural resource stocks, land and ecosystems, is often undervalued and mismanaged. This imposes costs to the economy and human well-being.*

- *The absence of coherent strategies to deal with these issues creates uncertainty, inhibits investment and innovation, and can thus slow economic growth and development.*

This underscores a need for better ways of measuring economic progress: measures to be used alongside GDP which more fully account for the role of natural capital in economic growth, human health and well-being.

While different country situations will demand different responses, clear and predictable policy signals to investors and consumers will deliver benefits from greening growth in the form of:

- *Economic gains from eliminating inefficiency in the use and management of natural capital.*

- *New sources of growth and jobs from innovation and the emergence of green markets and activities.*

The gains from growth, while distributed unevenly around the world, have been dramatic. Over the past 150 years life expectancy increased by around thirty years in most regions, including some of the least developed parts of the world. OECD countries experienced a three-fold increase in both the amount of time and money spent on leisure since the late nineteenth century, while health status and education and labour market opportunities also grew.[1]

Many of the economic, technological, social, and institutional changes that helped to drive growth in the twentieth century are yet to be delivered to a vast number of people. There is therefore considerable potential for further growth and improvements in living standards. The question is whether this potential can be realised.

The growth dynamic that has yielded these improvements in living standards has entailed substantial costs to the physical environment on which human well-being ultimately depends. It is increasingly apparent that the way in which we use natural resources could place higher living standards and even conventionally measured growth at risk.

In the 20th century the world population grew 4 times, economic output 22 times and fossil fuel consumption 14 times (UNEP, 2011). The resilience of a wide range of environmental systems is now being tested by the requirements of a rapidly growing global population and increased levels of economic activity. This includes meeting the energy and food needs of 9 billion people in 2050. Water supplies are coming under increasing pressure and, without new policy action a further 1 billion people are expected to live in severe water-stressed areas by 2030 (Figure 1.1).

Thus the world faces twin challenges: expanding economic opportunities for a growing global population; and addressing environmental pressures that, if left unaddressed, could undermine our ability to seize these opportunities. Green growth is where these two challenges meet and about exploiting the opportunities which lie within. It is about fostering economic growth and development while ensuring that natural assets continue to provide the resources and environmental services[2] on which our well-being relies. It is also about fostering investment and innovation which will underpin sustained growth and give rise to new economic opportunities.

Greening the growth path of an economy depends on policy and institutional settings, level of development, resource endowments and particular environmental pressure points. There is no "one-size-fits-all" prescription for implementing a green growth strategy. Advanced, emerging, and developing countries will face different challenges and opportunities in greening growth, as will countries with differing economic and political circumstances. There are, on the other hand, common considerations that need to be applied in all settings. And in every case, policy action requires looking across a very wide range of policies, not just explicitly "green" (*i.e.* environmental) policies.

Figure 1.1.   Key environmental challenges

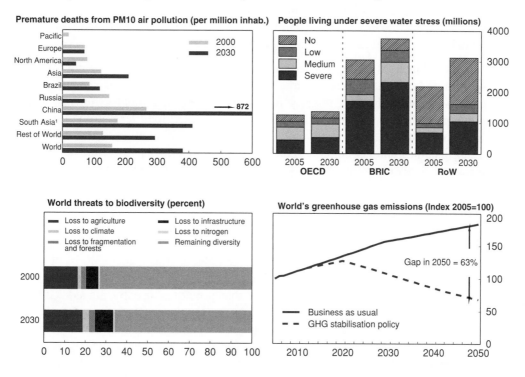

1.   Including India.

Source: OECD (2008), *Environmental Outlook to 2030*, and OECD (2009), *The Economics of Climate Change Mitigation: Policies and Options for Global Action beyond 2012.*

StatLink ⌐⌐⌐⌐ http://dx.doi.org/10.1787/888932422040

Underpinning this strategy is a framework for growth which is adapted to account for some of the shortcomings in conventional growth frameworks (Box 1.1). The starting point is that boosting growth means improving the quantity and quality of factors of production, and putting them to more productive use. These sources of growth remain the same whether or not we take account of environmental considerations. But the strategy explicitly recognises the dual role played by natural capital in both contributing to production of marketable goods and directly providing valuable ecosystem services to individuals and society at large.

The overarching goal of the framework is to establish incentives or institutions that increase well-being by: improving resource management and boosting productivity; enticing economic activity to take place where it is of best advantage to society over the long-term; leading to new ways of meeting these first two objectives, *i.e.* innovation. This requires drawing on mutually reinforcing aspects of environmental and economic policy. At the same time, some fundamental differences between these two policy domains need to be bridged. In markets the interaction of large numbers of producers and consumers and competition are an immensely powerful force for uncovering and creating value, driving productive efficiency, and rewarding creativity. However, when it comes to market decisions relating to the use of natural capital (and to some extent government decisions), these are influenced by payoffs which do not fully reflect the value of the entire asset base of the economy. Properly valuing natural capital is therefore an essential part of any green growth strategy. Properly valuing non-market benefits and costs, such as those related to health and life expectancy, will also be important when assessing policy options.

This framework will need to account for major social impacts of natural asset losses. Hence it will also involve achieving smooth and just adjustment in labour markets by ensuring that workers have the means to find opportunity in change. More generally, the success of a green growth strategy will rest on addressing political obstacles and distributional concerns about the costs of change.

Poverty reduction objectives will also need to be addressed in adapting this framework to emerging and developing countries, with the aim of identifying synergies with green growth objectives. The greening of growth can contribute to poverty reduction by bringing more efficient infrastructure to people (*e.g.* in energy and transport) and by underpinning sustained long-term growth. It can contribute by alleviation of poor health associated with environmental pollution. And given the centrality of natural assets in providing incomes and economic opportunities to the world's poorest people, it can minimise the risks of a legacy of costly environmental degradation as development proceeds.

Reframing growth

The central feature of a green growth framework (Box 1.1) is recognition of natural capital as a factor of production and its role in enhancing well-being. Simple as this statement is, it has important implications for economic policy and the way we evaluate economic growth. A number of these can be highlighted by reflecting on shortcomings in the way that growth is usually judged. GDP remains an essential metric for understanding economic performance. However, it does not necessarily reflect changes in capital stocks, or wealth, which are key determinants of both current and future growth and welfare gains. If production is based on the liquidation of assets, then it can be increasing while wealth is declining. Indeed, in recent years, wealth in a number of economies from across the developmental spectrum has been declining even as output has increased (Figure 1.2). This could undermine future growth potential.

Figure 1.2.   Rising GDP and declining wealth in some countries

1990-2005

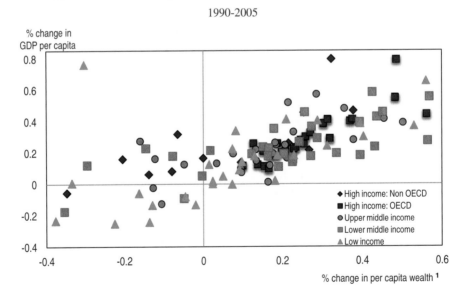

1.   The wealth estimates incorporate stocks of manufactured, human, social and natural capital. Measured natural capital in these data include agricultural land, protected areas, forests, minerals, and energy but exclude a range of assets which are difficult to measure and value including water resources.

Source: Based on data from World Bank (2010), *The Changing Wealth of Nations: Measuring Sustainable Development in the New Millennium.*

Ideally, strategies for growth should take account of all types of capital: natural (*e.g.* ecosystems), human (*e.g.* education and skills), physical (*e.g.* machinery and equipment), and the intangible assets which are so crucial to human progress like ideas and innovation. Accounting for growth in this way can produce quite different results compared to growth more conventionally defined.[3]

Perceived trade-offs between economic growth and environmental protection are attenuated when new measures that better capture well-being are used alongside GDP to measure progress. For many years GDP has been taken as a reasonable indicator of such material well-being and even as a proxy for the quality of life more broadly. But there is now an important debate about whether this is still a useful approximation.[4]

Natural capital, encompassing natural resource stocks, land and ecosystems, is often undervalued and mismanaged. Even where outputs derived from its exploitation are priced in markets, the scarcity of natural resource stocks may not be fully reflected in the value of goods and services arising from their exploitation. Identifying and addressing where this is the case presents opportunities for improvements in efficiency that constitute net gains for society.

Undervaluing natural capital also has implications beyond economic inefficiency because, much like human capital, it contributes to both growth and the quality of growth with respect to human welfare. These contributions, such as the benefits of clean air to human health, are not fully taken into account when the value of natural capital and the services it provides are not fully priced in markets (Box 1.2).[5]

The need to reframe growth is becoming increasingly important due to imbalances being created by the impacts of economic activity on environmental systems. In many cases, substituting physical for natural capital is becoming increasingly costly. Limited substitution possibilities between natural and physical capital and the fact that the quality of natural capital can change abruptly also introduces the potential for bottlenecks which can choke off growth. Current commodity price strength, including food prices, is perhaps a case in point at the global level.

Furthermore, changes in natural ecosystems can occur quickly and drastically (as has happened to some fish stocks) leading to (unexpected) growth reversals. Attention to the natural asset base brings into sharp relief some of the risks to growth from mismanaging natural capital and undermining the productivity of natural systems, especially systemic risks exemplified by climate change and biodiversity loss.

The absence of coherent strategies to deal with these dynamic issues can place a further drag on growth because of uncertainty about future regulatory conditions that inhibit private sector initiatives and investments in greener growth opportunities. Such effects are likely to be especially pronounced in the current economic climate.

In addition, economic and policy decisions have long-lived consequences due to the slowly evolving nature of the physical capital stock. Indeed current patterns of growth, consumer habits, technology and infrastructure all reflect an accumulation of past innovations and also past incentives that misguide behaviour, partly reflecting inappropriate government policies. Inefficiencies referred to earlier are to some extent hard-wired into the way economies function. This "path dependency" may continue to exacerbate systemic environmental risks and economic inefficiencies even after more basic valuation and incentive problems have been addressed.

In this regard, a key element of any green growth strategy is to set incentives that will boost innovation along a growth trajectory which diverts from inefficient patterns of the past. In this context, sound economic policy, robust competition and private sector innovation remain central drivers of growth and necessary conditions for unleashing new economic opportunities. Similarly, labour market conditions and educational opportunities need to be supportive of emergent industries and structural change.

In sum, strategies for greening growth focus on a broader concept of progress than just GDP growth and aim to provide clear and stable policy signals to investors and consumers so as to:

- Achieve economic gains from eliminating sources of inefficiency in the use of natural capital.

- Encourage innovation which can deliver high rates of balanced growth.

- Foster new economic opportunities from the emergence of new green markets and activities.

- Ensure that eliminating inefficiencies, fostering innovation and seizing new growth opportunities avoid the risk of bottlenecks and systemic crises.

The next two sections explore these dimensions in more detail.

Box 1.1.   A framework for thinking about green growth

Economic growth is conventionally thought of as the process through which workers, machinery and equipment, materials and new ideas and technologies contribute to producing goods and services that are increasingly valuable for individuals and society. A framework for thinking about green growth builds on this with four additional elements:

- Capturing the importance of changes in the comprehensive wealth of an economy. That means attention to all types of capital: natural (*e.g.* ecosystems), human (*e.g.* education and skills), physical (*e.g.* machinery and equipment), and the intangible assets which are so crucial to human progress like ideas and innovation. This captures some important aspects of growth including the nature of tradeoffs which arise at the frontier of production possibilities. For example, substituting environmental assets in production or consumption is not necessarily a smooth process: critical thresholds can be crossed after which assets that are renewable cease to be so (*e.g.* fisheries or soil) or assets that are non renewable are depleted to a point that substitution with other inputs or goods and services becomes impossible (*e.g.* climate or biodiversity), potentially short-circuiting growth in well-being. This introduces uncertainties about thresholds, irreversible outcomes and discontinuities that complicate policy design.

- Incorporating the dual role played by natural capital in this process. Natural capital contributes to production by providing crucial inputs, some of which are renewable and others which are not. It also influences individual and social welfare in various ways, through the effect that the environment has on health, through amenity value and through provision of ecosystem services.

- Acknowledging that investment in natural capital is an area in which public policy intervention is most needed because market incentives are weak or non-existent. This is largely because the contribution of natural capital to production is often not priced and the contribution of natural capital to individual welfare is not appropriately valued. The lack of proper valuation and market incentives or signals can affect behaviour and truncate the foresight of households and firms in ways that set the economy on trajectories that are unsustainable (or conversely that miss growth opportunities) or that are not necessarily maximising well-being. This means that in many cases, better management of natural capital (*e.g.* via proper valuation of pollution) will be consistent with higher GDP and a lower environmental impact of economic activities. A clear example is when an inefficient energy mix (involving excessive use of fossil fuels) is improved upon by eliminating harmful fossil fuel subsidies.

- Recognition that innovation is needed to attenuate tradeoffs that arise between investing in (depleting) natural capital and raising consumption or investing in other forms of capital. Indeed, once resource productivity is raised and inefficiency eliminated a "frontier" is reached along which these tradeoffs become more pronounced. Through innovation, the frontier at which tradeoffs start to bind can be pushed outwards; essentially greening growth.

Integrating these elements into policy is at the heart of green growth. In terms of well-being, policy decisions need to reflect the relative value to households of services from natural capital relative to other goods, and thus the tradeoffs that occur at the frontier. Tradeoffs need to be evaluated and re-evaluated over time to weigh the impacts of a decline in natural capital for current and future generations. These tradeoffs vary geographically depending on available technologies, the natural resource base and on households' and societal preferences; hence, policies have to be adapted to different circumstances.

From a production perspective, an assessment needs to be made of the extent to which natural capital can be depleted and replaced by other forms of capital. Different considerations will apply for different environmental assets (*e.g.* renewables and non-renewables); there is no single rule for determining whether assets should be preserved or not.

Most importantly, policies that aim to push out the frontier of economic growth need to grapple with existing incentives to innovate which are heavily biased towards improving the efficiency of currently dominant production techniques (e.g. in energy and transport) due to the tendency of innovation to build on previous innovations and existing technologies. Overcoming this kind of "path dependency", which contributes to inhibit the development of green technology (other factors are learning-by-doing effects and economies of scale) through appropriate innovation policies is therefore crucial for green growth.

Green growth dividends

Servicing higher living standards for 9 billion, increasingly urban, and increasingly wealthy, people will mean massive expansion in the markets for goods and in investment demand, especially for buildings and network infrastructure. On the current trajectory, global agricultural production will need to increase by over 50% by 2030 to feed the rising number of people with changing dietary preferences and world primary energy use is expected to rise by over 54% (OECD, 2008a).

Under "business as usual", we would certainly see increased pollution, negative impacts on human health, and constraints on the improvement of living standards due to increasing prices of essential commodities like food and energy, though not at a rate that would be sufficient to spur greener behaviour without targeted policy intervention. In reality, business is never "as usual". Markets, societies, and policies are constantly changing. The rapid economic progress of the last 150 years saw periods of major technological and social change that some regarded as major risks, but that on balance turned out to be opportunities. We can reasonably expect that such changes will occur again, and again will generate opportunities.

Fostering new markets and activities

Aware of environmental and economic challenges, governments have already implemented policies or promulgated strategies to affect a shift towards cleaner production, to promote greener business practices and green innovation. But it must be kept in mind that achieving higher living standards depends not only on doing things differently, but also on doing them better. This depends much less on where resources flow through a "green" economy but rather how efficiently those resources are used by businesses.

Greener business practices will have important economic pay-offs in terms of resource efficiency. Many of these are in the energy sector or related to energy use. The International Energy Agency (IEA), for example, estimates that the 17% (USD 46 trillion) increase in energy investment required globally between 2010 and 2050 to deliver low-carbon energy systems would yield cumulative fuel savings equal to USD 112 trillion (IEA, 2010). Energy conservation is one of the first steps that some companies have taken to reduce their GHG emissions (OECD, 2010), as it often leads to cost reductions. By using less energy, for instance, Dow Chemicals saved some USD 9 billion over 15 years (Dow, 2010) and DuPont some USD 5 billion since 1990 (DuPont, 2010).

More generally, a number of companies seek competitiveness gains through clean technology investment. Realising that environmental performance will be a major competitive factor in the future, leading companies are increasingly finding innovative ways of mainstreaming sustainability considerations into their core business. For instance, in a survey of 300 top executives from large global corporations by Ernst & Young (2009), more than 75% of respondents project their annual clean energy technology spending to rise over the next five years.

New and improved technologies in energy production, such as solar power, biomass, micro-hydro power and biofuels, linked with new approaches to electricity generation and distribution, could reduce the costs and improve the technical feasibility of energy supply in poor developing countries and allow non-oil producing countries to become more energy self sufficient. They would also bring a range of benefits, including reduced dependence on fossil fuels, reduced poverty and lower energy bills for firms and households.

Environmental action also generates new business opportunities. For instance, firms see the search for environmental performance as an opportunity to gain advantage over less technologically advanced rivals and to capture market shares. In natural resource sectors alone, commercial opportunities related to environmental sustainability could be between USD 2.1 and 6.3 trillion by 2050 - assuming that sufficient changes are made to ensure that standards of living can be sustained within the limits of available natural resources and without further harm to biodiversity, climate and other ecosystems (WBCSD, 2010).

Business opportunities have also emerged from the sustainable use of biodiversity and ecosystem services including the global market for certified organic food which exceeds USD 30 billion. Valuable new biodiversity related asset classes have also emerged; in the United States for example, wetland banking credits range in value from USD 7 000 – 850 000 per hectare and have attracted substantial entrepreneurial investment (TEEB, 2010). There is arguably greater scope for economic growth in this sector.

New business models are also emerging. Energy-saving companies, for example, provide energy-saving solutions to other firms and public buildings. These firms are paid from the savings achieved, not by an up-front payment, facilitating the uptake of costly technologies. Other emerging business models include product service systems where the value proposition shifts more to the services delivered by products rather than the products themselves, such as car sharing schemes (EPA, 2009).

Raising resource efficiency to sustain growth

Mismanagement of natural assets leads to high economic costs for society. Examples of the cost of mismanagement are perhaps most stark in the case of resources with undefined or unenforced property rights, and incentives to "free-ride". Over-exploitation of fish stocks and groundwater are cases in which depletion frequently exceeds the natural rate of regeneration, involving significant associated costs of overuse:

- The World Bank (2007) has estimated that in China the cost of excessive use of groundwater was in the range of 0.3% of GDP, with those costs falling largely on the agricultural sector.

- In Mexico's coastal aquifer of Hermosillo, annual withdrawals three to four times the recharge rate resulted in a 30 meter drop in water tables and saltwater intrusion at the rate of 1 kilometre per year, causing large agribusiness firms to relocate to other regions. (World Bank, 2008).

- According to the USDA (2007), declining groundwater supplies were largely responsible for the loss of an estimated 1.435 million acres of irrigated cultivated cropland in the State of Texas between 1982 and 1997.

More generally, there is growing evidence of the costs of losses in ecosystem function (OECD, 2008b; TEEB, 2010). Existing loss of biodiversity and degradation of ecosystems has already had dramatic consequences for business. Soil erosion in Europe is estimated to cost EUR 53 per hectare per annum (EEA, 2005). In Ghana, it is estimated that soil erosion will cost around 5% of total agricultural GDP over the 10 years from 2006 to 2015 (Diao and Sarpong, 2007). Similar and some even larger impacts are reported for other countries (OECD, 2009b).

Loss of ecosystem services has strong negative effects on welfare and human capital. Impairment of human health through environmental degradation reduces well-being but not necessarily GDP (or only to the extent that impaired health reduces available labour resources and productivity) (Box 1.2). The negative impacts of uncontrolled pollution are large and often felt strongest in the developing world and amongst the most vulnerable. Water pollution has been estimated to be responsible for 1.7 million deaths annually, concentrated (90%) amongst children under 5 years old. Air pollution is estimated to lead to a loss of 6.4 million years of life each year (Cohen et al., 2004). On the other side of the coin, benefits can be considerable. In the United States the measurable public health benefits from the Clean Air Act in 2010 are estimated to be USD 1.3 trillion and outweigh related costs by a factor of 30 to 1 (USEPA,

2010). Annual economic losses caused by introduced agricultural pests in the United States, the United Kingdom, Australian, South Africa, India and Brazil exceed USD 100 billion (TEEB, 2010).

While clean-up after the fact is sometimes an option, preventing losses to ecosystem function is often significantly more cost-effective than remediation. In the United States and the European Union, for example, estimates of the costs of cleaning up contaminated soils and oil spills run into the billions (OECD, 2008b). And many developing countries may not have the means to pay for remediation. Moreover, while some environmental impacts may be potentially "reversible" – allowing for the restoration of environmental conditions to their prior state – there are many areas in which this is not the case – once degraded, environmental and economic values are lost permanently. Clear-cutting of primary forests and groundwater contamination are two examples.

A mixture of market and regulatory failures contribute to imperfect management of many natural assets. For instance, ecosystem services are often overlooked because they come at a limited cost or zero cost to producers even though the value of these services is in fact large, albeit difficult to measure (Box 1.2). For example, it has been estimated that the worldwide economic value of pollination services provided by insect pollinators (mainly bees), was EUR 153 billion in 2005 for the main crops that feed the world (Gallai *et al*, 2009). Accounting for the value of natural capital can help to avoid patterns of development that lock-in high costs or resource bottle-necks; such as urban development in metropolitan Mexico City which has locked-in demand for fresh water from distant lowland sources which has to be pumped at high cost.

Indeed, beyond the estimated costs, mismanagement of natural capital can lead to declining productive potential and bottlenecks that can choke off growth. Moreover, the dampening effect that inefficient resource use can have on growth is exacerbated by imperfections in markets associated with natural resources, such as transport and energy where the presence of natural monopolies, state control, or subsidies can worsen environmental damage and support inefficient economic activity. Better management of natural capital will help avoid some of the economic costs that arise from excessive demands on the environment, thereby improving growth prospects.

Box 1.2.   Valuing non-market benefits

In the presence of externalities and/or incomplete property rights the economic "value" of natural capital will not be fully reflected in the prices faced by agents in the market, and as a result the natural capital base will be over-exploited. In order to make choices about the optimal extent and rate of exploitation of resources, it is necessary to attach a value to changes in environmental conditions.

In economics, relative preferences are the principal source of value. For goods and services exchanged on markets, value is reflected in people's "willingness-to-pay" – the amount of money an individual is willing to pay for a good or service - or "willingness-to-accept" – the amount of money an individual is willing to accept as a compensation for foregoing a good or service. Where environmental assets are used directly, this source of value is generally well captured by markets. However, the value of environmental assets is not only in direct use, but also indirect (or non-consumptive) use and in "non-use". These latter values are the subject of much research and debate.

Direct use includes the acquisition of materials, energy or space for human activities; *e.g.* the value of timber from a forest or energy in an oil field. Indirect use, where the physical characteristics of an asset do not change, includes recreational use of a body of water and ecosystem services from waste assimilation, carbon sequestration, fish habitat, and flood control. Use values include the actual or planned use of the good or service in question (that is, as a source of water for irrigation purposes) or possible use (that is, a spawning ground for development of fisheries in the future). Non-use values incorporate those values which people attach to a good or service even though he or she does not have (or foresee) any actual, planned or possible, use for the good or service for him or herself. These include "existence" values which arise from a sense that the good or service should not cease to be (*i.e.* perhaps because the wetland supports the existence of a threatened species).

The notion of possible use is particularly important in the context of environmental irreversibilities. For example, once a wetland is converted to commercial property use, alternative possible uses are lost forever. The option is foreclosed – hence the term, option value.

For any given change in environmental conditions, direct use, indirect use and non-use values can, be aggregated into a "total economic value" (TEV) for society; albeit not without some practical difficulties and ambiguity, especially in terms of quantifying non-use and option values. Nonetheless all these sources of value remain important and are not fully counted by markets.

Non-market benefits also include improvements in health and life expectancy from pollution reduction. For example, Bollen *et al.* (2009) find that air pollution would be dramatically reduced following the reduction of GHG emissions by 50 %, resulting in substantial gains in life expectancy relative to a business-as-usual scenario. Using an index of economic progress (welfare) that combines the changes in GDP per capita and the value of living longer, Murtin and de Serres (2011) find that, on average, the estimated gains in life expectancy would halve the welfare loss associated with climate change mitigation cost (Figure 1.3). In China and India, this loss would be reduced by respectively 20% and 32%, and in developed economies such as Australia, Canada, Japan and New Zealand, by more than 80%. In the United States, large gains in life expectancy would overcome the monetary cost of climate change mitigation by a significant margin.

Figure 1.3   Health benefits from climate mitigation

Percentage points

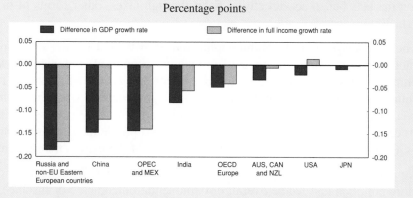

Source: Murtin, F and A. de Serres (2011), "Welfare Analysis of Climate Change Mitigation Policies", *OECD Economics Department Working Papers* (forthcoming).

StatLink 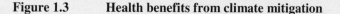 *http://dx.doi.org/10.1787/888932422059*

Appropriately valuing natural resources and ecosystem services is important for growth in all countries, because increased global trade, capital flows and the movement of people mean that issues manifesting themselves locally, such as waste management, can have international roots and vice versa. For instance, the capacity for domestic policies to have adverse effects internationally was highlighted by the role of biofuel support policies which, in conjunction with a number of other factors including bad weather and export restrictions, helped contribute to a rapid rise in world food prices between 2005 and 2008, which in turn created food crises in many parts of the developing world. More recently, commodity export restrictions have contributed to driving up food prices. Similarly, mismanagement of waterways can affect water quality and supply in other countries.

The relative importance of efficient use of natural capital is, however, much higher in some countries than others. In low-income countries, natural capital constitutes 25% of total per capita wealth, as compared to 12% in middle-income countries and 2% in OECD countries (World Bank, 2010b). Agriculture, which is dependent on fertile soil and availability of water, is Africa's largest economic sector generating over USD 100 billion annually and representing 15 percent of the continent's total GDP (McKinsey, 2010).

In resource-dependent countries, leveraging natural resources is also an important contributor to GDP. However, long-term growth prospects rest on reinvestment of some portion of the rents from natural asset depletion into physical capital such as infrastructure or into human capital through education or health care – essentially so that resource-led output growth is not undermining the overall asset base of the economy.

In areas where property rights can be attributed and enforced, activities that maintain the natural capital stock can be just as commercially attractive as those that damage the environment without the beneficiaries paying for the harm. In many places, however, the development of commercial activities to promote the preservation of forests and natural habitats may not be sufficiently attractive without properly pricing the negative externalities caused by logging and farming. Moreover, weak institutional arrangements and ineffective governance of natural resources often prevents maintenance of capital values.

Where property rights are enforced, markets have a capacity to react spontaneously to the gradual build-up of economic and environmental tensions that reduce resource productivity, such as resource scarcity and pollutants. But this will only happen where these pressures are reflected in prices or consumer demand and can be foreseen. Therefore the "appropriate response to substantial market failure is not to abandon markets but to act directly to fix it through taxes, other forms of price correction, or regulation" (Stern, 2009).

Translating better management of natural capital into growth will require economy-wide strategies encompassing not just green policies, as conventionally recognised, but also growth policies. The business environment needs to be conducive to adjustment and growth. Businesses are well aware of looming environmental challenges. Uncertainty about how governments will deal with these challenges will dampen investment both in cleaner production and investment more generally. There is also a risk that if policy proceeds in an ad hoc way, picking one or two problems to address through one or two policy responses, then it will be ineffective in addressing some of the major environmental risks.

Strategies are required to prevent resource efficiency improvements from leading to greater resource consumption, more pollution and worse overall environmental outcomes. For instance, this could occur due to so-called "rebound effects" where improvements in resource efficiency reduce the relative price of resources and people use more of them (*e.g.* more efficient heating resulting in warmer homes rather than lower energy use).

Systemic risks and imbalances

For a large number of countries, especially in the OECD, natural capital does not at a first glance appear to be a large part of the overall capital base of the economy and therefore is not a major contributor to growth. But this can be misleading because natural systems are complex and interdependent. Like institutions and networks, the value of natural systems is greater than the sum of the parts and their contribution to growth is essential.

Life adapts to varying amounts of water and nutrients in natural systems, and to the varying rates at which these essential materials are cycled. Leveraging one part of the system – speeding up the rate of natural flows or cycles – affects other parts of the system and imbalances can emerge. This raises risks to future growth as economic activity depletes and erodes natural assets at rates in excess of regeneration, threatening to undermine the regenerative balance or productive capacity of environmental systems. While an analogy with economic systems is necessarily incomplete, the crisis of 2007 and 2008 did illustrate that when systemic imbalances emerge, whether through excessive leverage and risk taking or some other means, they may be large and unexpected and they may not resolve themselves in an orderly fashion.

In natural systems, responses to stressors such as pollutants are non-linear. Fertiliser use, for example, can increase nitrogen levels in waterways to a point at which abrupt, non-linear changes occur in structure and function of ecosystems, *e.g.* excessive algae in surface waters and/or the loss of biodiversity including fish stocks. Bio-magnification of hazardous substances in the food chain can lead to concentrations in top predators (*e.g.* tuna) that are thousands of times those in the surrounding environment (*e.g.* the ocean), with consequent risks to human health of consumers.

Thresholds might manifest on a much larger scale. In the case of climate change, there may be a "tipping point" at which the thermohaline circulation of the oceans is disrupted, with significant negative implications for climate regulation in the northern hemisphere and the global economy. Other risks of tipping points could arise from deglaciation and ocean acidification. That said, it is important to recognise that there is not always broad-based consensus on where exactly critical limits lie from a scientific viewpoint. Rockström (2009) proposes a number of planetary boundaries based on the lower bound of estimated critical limits, and concludes that these boundaries have been crossed on climate change, biodiversity and the nitrogen cycle (Table 1.1).

Table 1.1. Planetary boundaries

Earth-system process	Parameters	Proposed boundary	Current status	Pre-industrial value
Climate change	*i) Atmospheric carbon dioxide concentration (parts per million by volume)*	350	387	280
	ii) Change in radiative forcing (watts per metre squared)	1	1.5	0
Rate of biodiversity loss	**Extinction rate (number of species per million species per year)**	10	>100	0.1–1
Nitrogen cycle (part of a boundary with the phosphorus cycle)	**Amount of N_2 removed from the atmosphere for human use (millions of tonnes per year)**	35	121	0
Phosphorus cycle (part of a boundary with the nitrogen cycle)	Quantity of P flowing into the oceans (millions of tonnes per year)	11	8.5–9.5	~1
Stratospheric ozone depletion	Concentration of ozone (Dobson unit)	276	283	290
Ocean acidification	Global mean saturation state of aragonite in surface sea water	2.75	2.90	3.44
Global freshwater use	Consumption of freshwater by humans (km_3 per year)	4 000	2,600	415
Change in land use	Percentage of global land cover converted to cropland	15	11. 7	Low
Atmospheric aerosol loading	Overall particulate concentration in the atmosphere, on a regional basis	To be determined		
Chemical pollution	For example, amount emitted to, or concentration of persistent organic pollutants, plastics, endocrine disrupters, heavy metals and nuclear waste in, the global environment, or the effects on ecosystem and functioning of Earth system thereof	To be determined		

Note: Boundaries for processes in bold have been crossed. A detailed description of the boundaries and the analysis behind them can be found in: www.stockholmresilience.org/download/18.1fe8f33123572b59ab800012568/pb_longversion_170909.pdf

Source: Rockström, J. et al. (2009), "A safe operating space for humanity", *Nature*, Vol. 461, 24 September 2009, pp. 472-475. Reprinted by permission from Macmillan Publishers Ltd, copyright 2009.

The uncertainty about when non-linear changes arise, the costs associated with them, and the irreversibility of such changes fundamentally alters the usual calculus of trade-offs.

There are two related aspects of greenhouse gas emissions that lead to irreversibility. On the one hand, the build up of greenhouse gases in the atmosphere is in large part irreversible due to the long lifetime of many greenhouse gases in the atmosphere. Once emitted, they can contribute to the stock of pollutants for over a century. On the other hand, some of the environmental damages that arise from a given stock of pollutants can be irreversible. While uncertainty exists about the precise timing and magnitude of damages, once they become fully known it will be largely impossible to avoid them.

Irreversibility or inertia also exists in the capacity of markets to adapt to a changing climate. Many important infrastructural assets which are carbon intensive are also very long lived. This raises the risk of being locked into growth with high environmental impact from which it will be very costly to change.

Business-as-usual growth in global greenhouse gas (GHG) emissions implies an increase of about 70% between now and 2050 with continued growth thereafter (OECD, 2009a). While the Cancun Agreements laid down a shared long-term vision which recognises a need to keep increases in global average temperature below 2° C and provided the foundations for meaningful long-term global action, uncertainty about the level of ambition and domestic political constraints remains a challenge. To meet this target, carbon productivity globally needs to increase ten-fold. To achieve that while maintaining standards of living implies large-scale innovation and structural economic change.

The costs of breaching the 2° C threshold may be large. This includes substantial destruction of physical capital through more intense and frequent storms, droughts and floods, for example from a rise in sea level and storm surge in heavily populated coastal areas (Nicholls *et al.*, 2008). The estimated costs of these impacts vary widely by location and region, but may be as much as the equivalent of 14.4% of per capita consumption when all market and non-market impacts are taken into account (Stern, 2006).

Biodiversity loss is also an instructive case of extreme uncertainty or indeed ignorance. Without more ambitious policy, a considerable number of today's known animal and plant species are likely to become extinct. Biodiversity loss is expected to continue, with particularly significant losses expected in Asia and Africa, and the loss of species as yet un-catalogued is, by definition, unknowable.

In the longer term, continued loss of biodiversity is likely to limit the Earth's capacity to provide the ecosystem services such as carbon sequestration, water purification, protection from extreme meteorological events, and the provision of common genetic material that support economic growth and human well-being.

The management of systemic risks will be viewed differently depending on whether the focus is on a single industry, the stewardship of an economy at large, or even the global economy. From an economy-wide perspective, there are clear downsides to acting too slowly. Priorities will vary depending on local environmental and developmental context. In low income countries, local health and environmental problems may take precedence over other issues such as the amenity value of local biodiversity or perhaps even damage from climate change.

Tensions exist between when to act and where to act and there is doubtless a trade-off between taking on adjustment today and taking it on tomorrow: act too slowly and the costs of inaction are high; too fast and the costs of action are high. There may be uncertainty about the optimal means and timing of interventions, since many of the investments undertaken are "sunk", embodied in long-live capital stocks and infrastructure. Taking rapid action in the short term to shift to low-carbon economies implies a degree of irreversibility and opportunity cost, to the extent that there is, at least hypothetically, some value in waiting for further information about the severity of the impacts or availability of new abatement technologies. These considerations, however, must be weighed against the potential for extreme non-linear, possibly catastrophic, changes to natural and human systems. Policies can influence the trade-offs (Jamet and Corfee-Morlot, 2009). With respect to climate change, adaptation will limit damages, and the risk of irreversible, catastrophic damage justifies action through the use of cost-effective policies even if the marginal costs exceed the margin benefits of action.

Notes

[1] Data from Maddison (2011), United Nations (1999), Kling and Shulz (2009) and Fogel (2004).

[2] For the purpose of this report, "environmental services" are defined as all services or functions provided by natural assets, and which contribute directly and indirectly to human well-being. This includes the provision of water, energy, raw materials, land and ecosystem inputs to produce goods and services, the regulatory capacity of the environment, and its roles in supporting life and biodiversity, and in providing amenities and cultural benefits. Environmental services are also referred to as "ecosystem services".

[3] For instance, Jones and Klenow (2010) show that adding health, leisure and inequality to the definition of well-being can lead to significant differences in the ranking of world countries and in growth rates of this more comprehensive measure than GDP.

[4] See for instance Stiglitz, Sen and Fitoussi (2009).

[5] Furthermore, environmental improvement which raises health status can increase labour force productivity and lift the rate of growth.

References

Bollen, J., B. Guay, S. Jamet and J. Corfee-Morlot (2009), "Co-Benefits of Climate Change Mitigation Policies: Literature Review and New Results", *OECD Economics Department Working Papers*, No. 693, OECD, Paris.

Cohen, A.J., H. R. Anderson, B. Ostro, K. D. Pandey, M. Krzyzanowski, N. Künzli, K. Gutschmidt, C. A. Pope III, I. Romieu, J. M. Samet and K. R. Smith (2004), "Urban Air Pollution", in M. Ezzatti, A.D. Lopez, A. Rodgers and C.U.J.L. Murray (eds.), *Comparative Quantification of Health Risks: Global and Regional Burden of Disease due to Selected Major Risk Factors*, Vol. 2, World Health Organization, Geneva, pp. 1353-1433.

Diao, X. and D. B. Sarpong (2007), "Cost Implications of Agricultural Land Degradation in Ghana; An Economy Wide Multimarket Model Assessment", *IFPRI Discussion Paper,* No. 00698, International Food Policy Research Institute, Washington DC.

Dow (2010), "Dow Sustainability Report: Global Reporting Initiative Report", The Dow Chemical Company, Michigan, available at www.dow.com/commitments/pdf/2015_SustainRep_3Q10.pdf.

DuPont (2010), "Case Study: Improving Energy Efficiency and Profitability with DuPont", DuPont Sustainable Solutions, Delaware, available at: www2.dupont.com/DuPont_Sustainable_Solutions/en_US/assets/downloads/DuPont_Energy_Efficiency_Case_Study.pdf.

EEA (European Environment Agency) (2005), "Market-Based Instruments for Environmental Policy in Europe", *Technical Report,* No. 8/2005, European Environment Agency and Office for Official Publications of the European Communities, Luxembourg.

EPA (2009), "'Green Servicizing' for a More Sustainable US Economy: Key Concepts, Tools and Analyses to Inform Policy Engagement", US Environmental Protection Agency, Office of Resource Conservation and Recovery, Washington DC.

Ernst & Young (2009), "Cleantech Matters, Going Big: the Rising Influence of Corporations on Cleantech Growth" , Ernst & Young, London.

Fogel, R. (2004), *The Escape from Hunger and Premature Death, 1700-2100: Europe, America, and the Third World*, Cambridge University Press, New York.

Gallai, N., J.M. Salles, J. Settele and B.E. Vaissière (2009), "Economic Valuation of the Vulnerability of World Agriculture Confronted with Pollinator Decline", *Ecological Economics*, Vol. 68, No. 3, Elsevier, Amsterdam, pp. 810-821.

IEA (2010), *Energy Technology Perspectives*, OECD/IEA, Paris.

Jamet, S. and J. Corfee-Morlot (2009), "Assessing the Impacts of Climate Change: A Literature Review", *OECD Economics Department Working Papers*, No. 691, OECD, Paris.

Jones, C.I. and P. J. Klenow (2010), "Beyond GDP? Welfare across Countries and Time," *NBER Working Papers,* No. 16352, NBER, Cambridge, Massachusetts, available at http://ideas.repec.org/p/nbr/nberwo/16352.html.

Kling, A. and N. Schulz (2009), *From Poverty to Prosperity: Intangible Assets, Hidden Liabilities and the Lasting Triumph over Scarcity*, Encounter Books Publishing, New York.

Maddison, A. (2011), "Angus Maddison 1926-2010", access at www.ggdc.net/maddison.

McKinsey & Company (2010), *McKinsey on Africa: A Continent on the Move*, McKinsey & Company, New York, available at www.mckinsey.com/clientservice/Social_Sector/our_practices/Economic_Development/Knowledge_High lights/~/media/Reports/SSO/Africa_FULL_VF.ashx.

Murtin, F and A. de Serres (2011), "A Welfare Analysis of Climate Change Mitigation Policies", *OECD Economics Department Working Papers,* OECD, Paris (forthcoming).

Nicholls, R., S. Hanson, C. Herweijer, N. Patmore, S. Hallegatte, J. Corfee-Morlot, J. Chateau and R. Muir-Wood (2008), "Ranking Port Cities with High Exposure and Vulnerability to Climate Extremes: Exposure Estimates", *OECD Environment Working Papers*, No. 1, OECD, Paris.

OECD (2008a), *Environmental Outlook to 2030*, OECD, Paris.

OECD (2008b), *Costs of Inaction on Key Environmental Challenges*, OECD, Paris.

OECD (2009a), *The Economics of Climate Change Mitigation: Policies and Options for Global Action beyond 2012*, OECD, Paris.

OECD (2009b), "Natural Resources and Pro-Poor Growth: The Economics and Politics", *DAC Guidelines and Reference Series*, OECD, Paris.

OECD (2010), *Transition to a Low-Carbon Economy: Public Goals and Corporate Practices*, OECD, Paris.

Rockström, J., W. Steffen, K. Noone, A. Persson, F. S. Chapin, III, E. F. Lambin, T. M. Lenton, M. Scheffer, C. Folke, H. J. Schellnhuber, B. Nykvist, C. A. de Wit, T. Hughes, S. van der Leeuw, H. Rodhe, S. Sörlin, P. K. Snyder, R. Costanza, U. Svedin, M. Falkenmark, L. Karlberg, R. W. Corell, V. J. Fabry, J. Hansen, B. Walker, D. Liverman, K. Richardson, P. Crutzen and J. A. Foley (2009), "A Safe Operating Space for Humanity", *Nature*, Vol. 461, 24 September 2009, Macmillan Publishers Limited, London, pp. 472-475.

Stern, N. (2006), *Stern Review: The Economics of Climate Change*, Cambridge University Press, Cambridge.

Stern, N. (2009), *A Blueprint for a Safer Planet: How to Manage Climate Change and Create a New Era of Progress and Prosperity*, Bodley Head, London.

Stiglitz, J. E., A. Sen and J. Fitoussi (2009), *Report by the Commission on the Measurement of Economic Performance and Social Progress*, available at www.stiglitz-sen-fitoussi.fr/en/index.htm.

TEEB (2010), *The Economics of Ecosystems And Biodiversity - Report for Business*, UNEP, Bonn.

UNEP (2011), *Decoupling and Sustainable Resource Management: Scoping the Challenges*, UNEP, Paris (forthcoming).

United Nations (1999), "The World at Six Billion", Document No. ESA/P/WP.154, 12 October 1999, United Nations, New York.

USDA (United States Department of Agriculture) (2007), "Long Range Planning For Drought Management - The Groundwater Component", USDA's Natural Resource Conservation Service, Washington DC, available at http://wmc.ar.nrcs.usda.gov/technical/GW/Drought.html.

USEPA (United States Environmental Protection Agency) (2010), *The Benefits and Costs of the Clean Air Act: 1990 to 2020,* Revised Draft Report, USEPA, Washington DC.

WBCSD (World Business Council on Sustainable Development) (2010), *Vision 2050: The New Agenda for Business*, WBCSD Publications, Geneva, available at www.wbcsd.org/web/projects/BZrole/Vision2050-FullReport_Final.pdf.

World Bank (2007), *Cost of Pollution in China: Economic Estimates of Physical Damages*, The World Bank, Washington DC.

World Bank (2008), *World Development Report 2008: Agriculture for Development*, The World Bank, Washington DC.

World Bank (2010a), *The Changing Wealth of Nations: Measuring Sustainable Development in the New Millennium*, The World Bank, Washington DC.

World Bank (2010b), *Trade Adjustment Costs in Developing Countries: Impacts, Determinants and Policy Responses*, The World Bank, Washington DC.

Chapter 2. Policy framework for green growth

Policies for greening growth will differ across countries, according to local environmental and economic conditions, institutional settings and stages of development. However, in all cases they need to: (i) integrate the natural resource base into the same dynamics and decisions that drive growth; (ii) develop ways of creating economic payoffs which more fully reflect the value of the natural resource base of the economy; and (iii) focus on mutually reinforcing aspects of economic and environmental policy.

This includes changing payoffs through:

- ***Pricing pollution and natural resource use** through mechanisms such as taxes or tradable permits. These are amongst the most cost-effective policy instruments. They incentivise efficiency gains and innovation. Crucially, they also generate revenue to help finance education, health care, infrastructure development or poverty alleviation. Time-limited subsidies can also be a useful tool for changing price signals; however they tend to be accompanied by higher costs.*

- ***Removing perverse subsidies** which encourage pollution or over-extraction of resources and place a drain on the public purse.*

- ***Ensuring that regulatory standards** focus on outcomes. Regulations that address pollution or energy efficiency can be important complements and effective substitutes for price-based policy. Information-based measures may also be needed to influence consumer and household behaviour and increase the effectiveness of other policy.*

Changing the payoffs in the economy is only part of the solution. Policy will also need to address inertia, the risks of technology lock-in, and the roles of innovation, infrastructure and institutions in enabling change:

- ***Innovation.** Government plays an important role in fostering green innovation. It can lend support by funding relevant research, supplying finance tailored to differing stages of technology development and using demand-side instruments such as standards, regulations and public procurement. Ensuring wide diffusion and international transfer of green technologies and practices is important. This requires reducing barriers to trade and foreign direct investment, effective protection and enforcement of intellectual property rights, and efforts aimed at the least developed countries.*

- ***Infrastructure investment programmes** in sectors such as water, energy, and transport. Well-planned programmes can help drive development, reduce water and air pollution, curb unsustainable land use change, and enable the deployment of next generation technologies. Financing these programmes needs to focus on leveraging private sector investment.*

- ***Institutional and governance capacity** to implement wide-ranging policy reform is an essential condition for greening growth. Governments need to integrate green growth objectives into broader economic policymaking, development planning and poverty reduction strategies.*

The pursuit of green growth will require a mix of measures that can collectively bolster growth, while guiding economic activity into modes of production and consumption with lower environmental impact. The key to this will be finding ways of integrating efficient natural resource use and other environmental considerations into every day economic decisions. In many cases, this will not entail new policies and a number of measures that will be needed are already in use.

Finding the right policy framework for growth has always been a challenge and integrating green growth does not make it less so. However, the experience of OECD countries, confirmed also by the experience of many emerging economies, suggests that while there is no single recipe for success, there are certainly some important ingredients. These include improving the quality of human capital through education and labour market policy, capital deepening assisted by sound macroeconomic policy, and more effective institutions that allow competition, innovation and entrepreneurship to flourish while protecting the social fabric and the rule of law.

Green growth strategies need to harness the creative power of markets and the insights from economic policy to integrate the natural resource base into the same dynamics and decisions that drive growth. A central element will be to develop ways of creating economic payoffs which more fully reflect the value of the natural resource base of the economy.

This chapter begins with a discussion of the main design dimensions for policy which are consistent with meeting the above objectives. Key policy instruments are then discussed. These form part of the policy toolkit for green growth (*Tools for Delivering on Green Growth*), albeit one which will vary according to different country circumstances. This includes discussion around options for reforming market prices through pricing instruments or retargeting government payments to encourage environmentally sound growth. It also touches on regulatory initiatives and other reforms necessary to support sustained long-term growth and innovation.

Changing the payoffs in the economy can, however, only be part of the solution given the inertia in economies and mismatches between private payoffs to economic decisions and social value. This has left an extraordinary challenge in changing the infrastructure of economies to avoid locking economic growth into a pathway that turns out to be regrettable. Infrastructure is an important ingredient in growth and arises out of a complex array of policy signals. Getting this part of the policy mix right will be crucial for greening growth. Similarly, consumers are to some extent locked into norms and habits of consumption and policy needs to reflect on ways of enabling consumer change. Innovation needs to be marshalled to help provide ways around old patterns of production and consumption and generate new sources of growth that better reflect the full value of economic activity to society. While better pricing of resource use and pollution, and smarter regulations, can help provide incentives for these shifts, more will be needed to overcome the inertia. Finally, new institutions and governance arrangements may be required to bring all these dimensions together in a coherent way and to overcome inertia in policy making practices.

Policy design[1]

Realising the value of the natural resource base in a way that is conducive to growth will entail modifying the payoffs to certain economic activities, adopting measures to overcome obstacles to green growth and implementing policies which directly improve environmental and economic outcomes from activity in natural resource sectors. The tools to do this will need to be drawn from a wide range of instruments (Table 2.1 contains examples of environmental policy instruments) and encompass a number of reforms.

Across the range of issues to be addressed, policy initiatives should be designed in terms of: cost-effectiveness, adoption and compliance incentives, and ability to cope with uncertainty and provide a clear and credible signal to investors. Other important criteria include effectiveness in stimulating innovation and the diffusion of green technologies, and the extent to which instruments can be designed and implemented in a way that facilitates international co-ordination.

It is also important to consider the extent to which policy is:

- robust, meaning that it is based on sound science and cost-benefit analysis;

- effective, ensuring that it is focussed on attaining environmental objectives;

- transparent, to provide stakeholders a voice, enable market certainty, reinforce credibility, and help engender public trust; and

- adaptable, with regular review and adjustment.

Table 2.1.   Environmental policy instruments

Policy instruments	Examples / Common applications
Cap-and-trade permit systems	- GHG emission reductions (EU-ETS)
	- Air pollution (SO_2, NO_x, VOC)
	- Fishing quotas and nutrient and water trading
Baseline-and-credit permit systems	- Clean Development Mechanism
	- Lead content of gasoline
	- Biodiversity offsets/banking (*e.g.* REDD)
Taxes or charges on pollution or resource use	- Water effluents
	- Water abstraction or consumption
Taxes or charges on a proxy (input or output)	- Fuels and coal
	- Motor vehicles
	- Fertilisers
	- Waste fees and levies
Subsidies	- Forest management and conservation
	- Purchase of environmental-friendly energy equipment
Deposit-refund systems	- Beverage and chemical containers
	- Lead acid batteries
Performance standards	- Limits on CO_2 emissions of a passenger vehicle
	- Energy efficiency standards for various manufactured goods.
Technology standards	- Minimum percentage of a low-carbon source in the overall fuel mix of passenger vehicle
	- Specific housing building codes for energy-saving purposes
Active technology support policies	- Feed-in tariffs for electricity generated by renewable sources
	- Renewable energy portfolio standard (green certificate)
	- Targeted public procurement
	- Loan guarantees and tax credits
Voluntary approaches	- Negotiated agreements to encourage energy efficiency in energy-intensive industries
	- Publicly-available inventories of various pollutants
	- Labelling schemes
	- Local municipal land use planning

The relative strengths and weaknesses of the different instruments with respect to those criteria, indicate that the best choice of instruments will vary by environmental issue as well as across country- or region-specific circumstances. Indeed, given the presence of several interacting market failures, the most appropriate green growth policy response will, in most cases, require a combination of instruments.

This combination will differ depending on a country's stage of development, its particular environmental concerns, political economy considerations, the importance of different natural assets to a country's growth prospects and social preferences. Market conditions will also need to be taken into account in policy design. For instance, intergenerational transfers that could improve the well-being of both current and future generations may fail to take place in countries with less-developed financial markets.

The introduction of green technologies in their early stages of development may have to be supported by specific measures to avoid path dependency built around "dirty" technologies. Furthermore, the design and implementation of policies often raises governance issues that differ across countries. Difficulties in monitoring environmental performance and compliance, collecting green taxes or setting up new markets may influence the choice of policy instruments in countries with large informal economies and where there is weak capacity in environmental policy design or implementation.

Distributional effects may play an equally important role in policy development. Politically successful measures will likely strike a balance between the above considerations and equity concerns by correcting for any adverse distributional impacts. For example, as discussed below, low-income households could receive various compensation mechanisms or cash payments.

Market instruments

For most countries, instruments that directly impact price signals are a necessary, though not always sufficient, condition for greening growth. The main strengths of market-based instruments is that, if well-designed, they modify price signals so that they internalise externalities (*e.g.* pollution) and that all factors of production, including natural capital, are properly valued. They can thus set the right incentives for broadly based actions that reduce environmental damage with the least resource cost, and also promote and guide "green" innovation (see *Tools for Delivering on Green Growth*: Table 4 for relative strengths and weaknesses of market-based instruments).

Taxes and permits

It is often said that "prices are not everything" with respect to environmental policies, suggesting that market-based instruments are widely used. In reality they are not. The use of market-based instruments to directly modify prices does not imply a single policy but an array of policy instruments of varying degrees of complexity. At their most simple, prices on large point source pollutants, such as large industrial installations, or on large scale resource use such as mining or water abstraction, are relatively simple to administer. At the other end of the spectrum are policies which target small, dispersed or hard-to-monitor activities. Capacity to deploy price-based instruments across this spectrum depends crucially on the country-specific institutional capacity and economic structure, as well as technological possibilities (*i.e.* monitoring). However, in the context of any policy package, market instruments to affect prices have a key role to play in most countries.

Pricing of environmental damage can be achieved through tradable permits or taxes. Properly designed and implemented they can be more or less equivalent. Tradable permit systems may stand a better chance of being defended by stakeholders once in place (though the authorities need to ensure that they do not impair competition by favouring existing firms and that they do not lead to speculation and fraud which significantly reduce their potential environmental benefits). They can involve steep start-up costs and price volatility in the early phases. Taxes are generally less complex to implement, but both taxes and permit systems entail potentially high monitoring and enforcement costs if applied directly to a pollution source whose emissions need to be measured with precision. While permit systems tend to work well when the control of emissions relates to relatively large emitters, taxation is likely to be more appropriate for small and diffuse sources of pollution such as households, farmers and small businesses.

A recent OECD study documents how Sweden's charge on NO_x emissions led plants to introduce a variety of abatement measures depending on what was most fit – and least costly – in each context (OECD, 2010a). New technical solutions also emerged, and a large number of patents were taken out by Swedish companies. If, instead, Sweden had mandated the use of particular technologies, it would not have given room for the development of new and better ways of cutting NO_x emissions – the scope for green growth would have been limited. In this sense, a tax on pollution works more with the logic of business: it gives a cost-advantage for businesses that bring down their pollution vis-à-vis competitors that do not do so. It also creates a market for entrepreneurs to develop and sell new smarter technologies for reducing pollution.

Economic efficiency requires that taxation targets the externality, implying that priority should be given to taxing pollution emissions directly. More commonly, taxes are applied on an input or output of a production process causing environmental degradation. These tend to be concentrated in the transport sector. Currently, around 90% of total revenues from environmental taxes are accounted for by taxes on motor vehicle fuels and motor vehicles in OECD on average (OECD, 2010b). Other examples include charges for water usage or waste collection and taxes on packages, pesticides and, more rarely, on fertilisers.

Box 2.1.   Green budget reform in action - the case of Germany

Many countries have implemented environmentally-related taxes (OECD, 2010a). In some countries, the cumulative implementation of different economic instruments for environmental management has amounted to important incentive and revenue effects. For instance, between 1999 and 2005, Germany introduced a set of environmental fiscal reform measures that, although not originally planned as such, amounted to possibly the largest integrated green budget reform in any country in the world. By 2005, Germany had altered financial incentives worth EUR 40-50 billion, or 2% of GDP, by (Goerres, 2006):

- Increasing most existing energy taxes, created a new electricity tax and introduced road tolls for trucks, generating EUR 22 billion

- Establishing CO_2 emissions trading for industrial and power generation plants covering some 57% of Germany's emissions (creating potential price effects of EUR 5-15 billion)

- Establishing a mandatory deposit regime for beverage packaging (creating financial incentives worth EUR 2-4 billion)

- Reducing some environmentally-harmful subsidies (such as tax relief for commuters) for EUR 4 billion

- Introducing subsidies for renewable energy and energy technologies for EUR 6 billion (to a large extent off-budget via power companies)

Source: OECD (2010), *Taxation, Innovation and the Environment*, and OECD (2011), "Draft Policy Guidance on Capacity Development for Environment" (forthcoming).

Importantly, market-based instruments can also play a role in growth-oriented tax reform. Depending on how far revenues from environmentally related taxes are in effect used to compensate losers, there is the potential to shift (part of) the burden away from more distortive corporate and personal income taxes and social contributions. Such a shift in the composition of taxes can promote economic growth, particularly if cuts are made in the elements of income taxes that are most distortive to investment, productivity growth and labour supply. For example, a permanent one-percentage point reduction of the average tax burden on labour is estimated to increase the employment rate by about 0.4 percentage points in the typical country over the long run (OECD, 2006a). Environmentally-related taxes are likely to be passed on into higher prices to some degree, so they may involve a reduction in real wages, in effect attenuating the scale of the reduction in the tax burden that may be attainable in practice (see OECD, 2010c). Much depends on the existing tax structure and how an income tax cut is implemented. However, most tax systems have room to improve incentives in income taxes and in ways that do not make the distribution of income less equal.

The use of environmentally related taxes and emission trading systems has widened over recent decades with a growing number of countries using taxes and charges in areas like waste disposal and on specific pollutants, such as emissions to air of NO_x and SO_x (Box 2.1). Meanwhile, the revenue from taxes on energy, which are the most widespread form of environmentally-related tax (Figure 2.1), has tended to decline as a share of GDP, partly because growing global energy demand has pushed up pre-tax prices and encouraged increased fuel efficiency – an illustration of the impact of economic incentives.

Figure 2.1.   Composition of environmentally related tax revenues by country

As a percentage of GDP in 2009

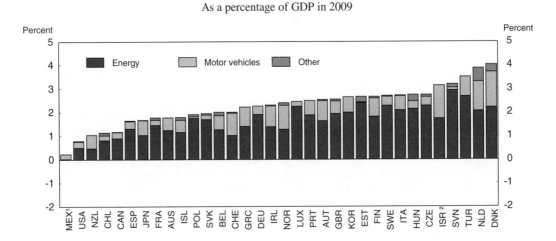

1. In Mexico, fluctuations of consumer prices on motor vehicle fuels are smoothed out. Since 2009, the Government is implementing a phase-out policy of inefficient fossil fuel subsidies. For Greece, a 2008 figure is used for motor vehicle taxes.

2. Information on data for Israel: see endnote 2.

Source: OECD/EEA database on instruments for environmental policy and natural resources management

StatLink *http://dx.doi.org/10.1787/888932422078*

In terms of the revenue-raising potential of environmentally related taxes, the biggest potential, by far, is from taxes related to energy and greenhouse gas emissions. Model simulations indicate that at a price of USD 50 per tonne of CO_2-equivalent greenhouse gas emissions (well below the level that many modelling exercises suggest might eventually be needed), revenues equalling 1-3% of GDP could be raised in 2020, depending on the circumstances in each country (Table 2.2).

Table 2.2.   Potential fiscal revenue from a CO_2 tax or an emission trading system

Revenue as % of GDP in 2020 following a gradual introduction covering all GHG emissions

Price on emissions per tonne of CO_2-equiv.	Australia and New Zealand	Canada	EU27 and EFTA	Japan and Korea	United States
USD 10	0.8	0.5		0.2	0.4
USD 25	1.9	1.2	0.7	0.5	1.0
USD 50	3.3	2.1	1.1	1.0	1.7
USD 100	5.7	3.6	2.3	1.7	2.9

Note: The simulation is based on scenarios in which all regions shown in the table act in tandem. The price on emissions shown in the table would be added on top of existing taxes, etc., except for the EU ETS which is included in the numbers.

Source: Simulations based on the OECD ENV-Linkages model.

While revenues from environmentally related taxes can only deliver a fraction of the fiscal consolidation needed in many countries, taxes on energy and CO_2 can be a natural part of a wider consolidation package (Figure 2.2). They are relatively easy to implement, and they may be an attractive alternative to higher taxes on labour or business income (given competitiveness concerns) or deep cuts in public expenditure (having regard to effects on human capital and social equity). Alternatively, fiscal consolidation can be based on other measures and followed by revenue-neutral green tax shifts at a later stage.

Following the economic crisis, a number of countries have used higher environmentally related taxes as part of their fiscal consolidation strategies. Ireland is a clear case where higher fuel taxes, the introduction of a CO_2 tax of EUR 15 per tonne (set to double to EUR 30 per tonne by 2014), and charges for water use comprise key elements in recent budgets. Given that many of the countries needing large fiscal consolidation collect relatively little revenue from taxes on energy, CO_2 and other pollutants, this may lead to convergence and less difference in environmental taxation across countries. For global environmental externalities such as climate change, convergence towards minimum prices on greenhouse gas emissions in all countries would be an ideal outcome that would resolve competitiveness concerns. Also, convergence towards more homogenous taxation of energy and CO_2 within regions of the world, such as among European countries, would mitigate concerns about competitiveness compared to today's more fragmented use of such market-based policies.

Charges for water supplied to farms have also been increasing in most OECD countries. Where countries have raised water charges, the available evidence indicates that it has improved water use efficiency. However, these charges and related policy measures rarely address the scarcity value of water nor do they reflect full cost recovery, especially with respect to capital costs of water supply infrastructure (OECD, 2010d).

In developing countries, there is also growing use of environmental levies, driven by the prospects of raising revenue and keeping it within the sector agencies. Such levies are often seen by environmental and natural resource agencies as a way to generate funding given low national budgetary allocations.[3] There are risks to this kind of earmarking. Public finance should provide for separation between revenue and expenditure initiatives. There are also environmental management and governance risks associated with the use of internally generated revenues in environment and natural resource agencies (Lawson and Bird, 2008).

Figure 2.2.   Fiscal consolidation and revenue from green taxes

As a percentage of GDP, 2008

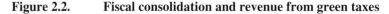

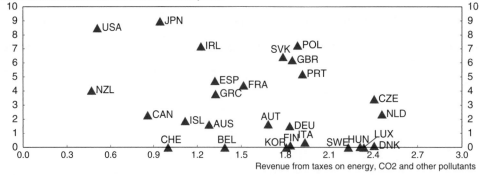

Note: The consolidation needs shown on the vertical axis are measured in terms of the required change in the underlying primary balance. They were estimated in the OECD Economic Outlook, No. 88, Figure 4.1, November 2010. Two other debt targets were also assessed: bringing government debt down to pre-crisis levels or to 60% of GDP, and both of these targets would imply larger consolidation than simply stabilising debt. The figures on the horizontal axis are the sum of the categories "energy" and "other" in Figure 2.1. All OECD countries are included for which data are available.

Source: OECD (2010), *Economic Outlook No. 88,* and OECD (2010), *Taxation, Innovation and the Environment.*

StatLink ⫯ℐℐ http://dx.doi.org/10.1787/888932422097

Implementing fiscal reforms for green growth can be a challenge in countries with a large informal economy *i.e.* limited tax collection capacity. In the forestry sector of Tanzania, it was estimated that USD 58 million was lost annually due to the under-collection of natural forest product royalties. A similar problem was detected in Tanzania's fishing sector with only 30% accruing to local government being collected (Schlegelmilch, 2007).

Despite these challenges, fiscal reforms present major potential for green growth, particularly when applied to natural resource management. For instance, water pollution charges in Chile brought USD 15 million to its environmental authorities between 1997 and 2000, and fishery access agreements in Guinea Bissau raise approximately 30% of government revenues (World Bank, 2005). Pricing of natural resources can be seen as an immediate win-win option to promote sustainable management of resources and increased fiscal revenue to the government.

Subsidies

Subsidies are a commonly used tool for shaping incentives. They can be an effective policy option when pricing instruments are too difficult or costly to enforce. Used in a targeted manner they can help shift the balance of incentives towards more environmentally-sound products and practices or to support new and immature technologies. Subsidies have also been common *e.g.* in the area of energy efficiency to enable low-income groups to gain from the economic benefits of conservation. These programs typically lower the up-front capital cost of investing in energy efficiency improvements, by offering grants, tax credits, or low-interest loans. For example, the *U.S. Low-Income Weatherization Program* was designed to help achieve energy conservation, while simultaneously aiding low-income residents with their energy bills.

However, subsidies involve complications around targeting, and how to find or redirect limited public funds. The demands that they place on governments in terms of administrative capacity and information requirements are considerable. Moreover, to be efficient, resistance to specific pleas from the affected sectors is necessary. Subsidies can have far-reaching and unintended consequences, but these are not always easily detected or visible to the public. This is the case for tax expenditures, which are often used to support fossil fuels in OECD countries, and of transfer payments and subsidies in agriculture.[4] As such, they require careful consideration in the context of green growth, including to ensure compliance with WTO obligations. At the same time, existing subsidies which run counter to the objectives of green growth policies need to be eliminated.

A range of subsidy programmes could be reviewed in this regard. Removing or reforming subsidies would, in many cases, increase the efficiency of economies and alleviate their potentially distortive effects on competition. This would help to free up public funds and boost green growth.

The IEA estimates that subsidies to fossil fuel consumption in 37 developing and emerging economies amounted to USD 557 billion in 2008 and USD 312 billion in 2009 (IEA, 2010a). There is significant scope for reducing the heavy burden that these subsidies place on government budgets, while also better targeting support to those who most need it. OECD analysis suggests that most countries or regions would record real income gains from unilaterally removing their subsidies to fossil fuel consumption, as a result of a more efficient allocation of resources across sectors (IEA, OPEC, OECD, World Bank, 2010). These real income gains could be as much as 4% in some countries (Figure 2.3). At the same time, global GHG emissions would be reduced by 10% in 2050 compared with business-as-usual (Figure 2.4).[5]

Figure 2.3.   Impact of unilateral removal of fossil fuel subsidies on real income

% deviation from baseline

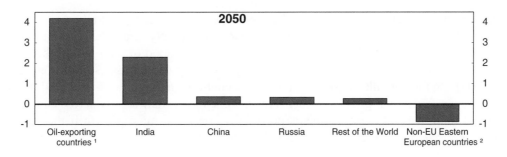

1. The region includes the Middle East, Algeria-Libya-Egypt, Indonesia and Venezuela.

2. This region includes Armenia, Azerbaijan, Belarus, Croatia, Georgia, Kazakhstan, Kyrgyzstan, Moldova, Tajikistan, Turkmenistan, Ukraine and Uzbekistan.

Source: OECD ENV-Linkages model based on IEA data.

StatLink ⟨⟨⟨ *http://dx.doi.org/10.1787/888932422116*

Savings from subsidy reform could offer a budgetary opportunity to boost support to green growth but this will depend on the local context. Subsidies on fossil fuels, for example, both encourage pollution and constrain the ability of governments to engage in programmes to boost long run growth through, for example, improved health and education. Subsidy reform may be most appropriately used as an opportunity to resolve these issues.

Figure 2.4.   GHG emissions with fossil fuel subsidy removals

% deviation from baseline

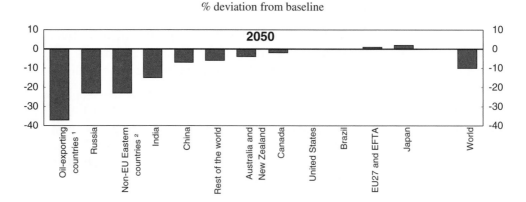

1. The region includes the Middle East, Algeria-Libya-Egypt, Indonesia and Venezuela.

2. This region includes Armenia, Azerbaijan, Belarus, Croatia, Georgia, Kazakhstan, Kyrgyzstan, Moldova, Tajikistan, Turkmenistan, Ukraine and Uzbekistan.

Source: OECD ENV-Linkages model based on subsidies data from IEA.

StatLink 🖳🖳 *http://dx.doi.org/10.1787/888932422135*

In natural resource sectors subsidies for large-scale harvesters are generally undesirable as they encourage wasteful use of resources. Moreover, they tend to negatively affect the economic opportunities of smaller scale harvesters or SMEs and adversely affect the livelihood of the poor. In the fishing sector subsidies are supporting continued investment in non-performing capital assets (Arnason, Kelleher and Willmann, 2008). In the agricultural sector, transfers account for nearly 1% of total GDP in the OECD. While this share has fallen over the last twenty-five years, it varies significantly across countries. In view of rising global food demand these payments potentially constrain green growth if they distort signals which would otherwise improve global agricultural productivity.

At the same time, targeted subsidies can support environmentally beneficial practices in the primary sector. There has, for example, been a decrease in the share of agricultural support that is linked to commodity production[6] and an increase in support measures conditional upon meeting environmental, food safety and animal welfare requirements; or support based on the generation of ecosystem services (*e.g.*, water purification, conservation of crop genetic diversity, provision of habitat for grassland birds). Thus the relationship between transfers and green growth in this sector is complex. Not all government transfers are harmful to growth and the environment; not all environmentally motivated subsidies are actually good for the environment; and the absence of transfers is no guarantee that environmental performance will be achieved.

De facto subsidies can also be a source of environmental harm. In the case of forestry, for example, log export bans or support for investment in processing capacity (with the intention of stimulating value-adding processing) can act as subsidies for domestic wood industries, even if timber extraction itself is not subsidised. The wood industry benefits from artificially low price of logs, increasing their incentive to over-harvest the woods. Economic analysis and case studies of Malaysia, Ghana and Indonesia have suggested that the main effect of logging bans has been to encourage overcapacity and maintain inefficiency in the wood-processing industry, both of which increase the pressure on forests (Porter, 2002).

In each case, as discussed in Chapter 3, the distributional effects of subsidy reform and environmental fiscal reform need to be examined carefully. Low income households can be vulnerable to these reforms as the percentage of their expenditure on water and energy is much higher compared to rich households; although the extent to which costs are born by the rich or the poor differs at country and regional levels. In the case of Indonesia's fossil fuel subsidy reform, for example, a targeted monthly payment was distributed to poor households to avoid unsustainable impacts on livelihoods (Beaton and Lontoh, 2010) (Box 2.2).

Box 2.2.   Fossil fuel subsidy reform in Indonesia

The Indonesian government joined the G20 pledge to phase out subsidies for fossil fuels, and a complete removal has been announced for 2014. In addition, the government plans a gradual reduction of total subsidies by 15% on average per year from 2011 to 2014.

Subsidies on energy consumption, and to a lesser extent on production, were introduced in Indonesia in order to make energy affordable for people on low incomes. However, they entail significant economic and environmental costs; they put pressure on the public budget and benefit mostly rich households.

Over-consumption of cheap energy increases Indonesia's dependency on energy imports. Subsidies can also reduce investment in new infrastructure and production processes, and prevent resources being used to achieve social outcomes. They can discourage competition and innovation, "lock-in" inefficient technologies, and make public spending more vulnerable to global energy movements. Fuel consumption tends to increase with income levels, and so the benefits of cheaper energy are mainly felt by high-income groups, while the cost is spread across the whole population. In 2008, the Co-ordinating Ministry of Economic Affairs advised that the top 40% of families receive 70% of the subsidies, while the bottom 40% benefit from only 15% of the subsidies.

The removal of energy subsidies would reduce energy use and lower GHG emissions, while leading to an improvement in the quality of life through better health outcomes. It is also expected to have significant general equilibrium effects, including on energy prices, consumption and trade. Efficiency gains are likely to benefit the economy as a whole. These impacts depend to a large extent on whether the subsidy removal is compensated through an increase in spending or through tax cuts.

The resulting spare resources could be efficiently used through direct income support, for instance targeted cash transfers to protect low-income households from attendant energy price rises. These transfers have been found to be more effective than subsidy policy in helping to boost incomes of the poorest segments of the population. Increasing subsidised energy prices would also facilitate the financing of additional spending on health, education and infrastructure (de Mello, 2010; Pisu, 2010), which are crucial to raising living standards in the longer term.

Source: Mourougane, A. (2010), "Phasing Out Energy Subsidies in Indonesia", *OECD Economics Department Working Papers,* No. 808.

Regulations and the regulatory environment

Regulatory policies affect the direction of growth so they are crucial elements of the green growth policy framework. As with the reform of subsidies, regulatory initiatives present an opportunity to both incentivise green growth and to improve existing arrangements. They are also needed to complement and support market-based instruments.

Particular areas where regulatory settings enable or impede green growth include: *i)* specific regulatory initiatives to encourage improved resource use, such as energy efficiency, and to reduce pollutants, such as emissions performance standards, *ii)* product market competition, *iii)* rules governing trade and foreign direct investment (FDI), *iv)* regulations enabling or impeding private sector voluntary initiatives, and *v)* procedural oversight to promote policy coherence and regulatory certainty.

Regulatory instruments, such as performance and technology standards, are often used when markets do not provide price signals to individuals or organisations that reflect the costs of behaviour (see *Tools for Delivering on Green Growth*: Table 5 for relative strengths and weaknesses of non-market instruments). This can be the case where pollution, for example, cannot be adequately monitored at the source – at least not at a reasonable cost – and there is no good proxy that could be subject to taxation. Emission of NO_x from motor vehicles is an example. In such a case, the imposition of performance standards can prove to be a good substitute for price-based instruments, provided that the enforcement of standards can be reliably verified. The efficiency of performance standards can be further enhanced if obligations are "tradable", allowing individual firms and households to trade-off the benefits and costs according to their particular circumstances. The case of tradable "white" (energy efficiency) certificate schemes introduced in Italy and elsewhere is one such example.

In general, such instruments should, to the extent possible, be designed around enhancing firm performance, in terms of resource efficiency or pollutant intensity.[7] Regulations which mandate the use of a particular technology have major drawbacks in terms of efficiency because they are inflexible and provide low incentives to innovate. However, technology standards can be the best option in specific circumstances, notably when the administrative costs of performance standards are too high and/or when abatement costs are relatively homogeneous across agents.

Overall, regulatory instruments have drawbacks relative to pricing instruments because they fail to provide an intrinsic mechanism for ensuring that environmental targets be attained at the least economic cost. Indeed, by concentrating action on the supply-side, non-market instruments need to over-compensate for the absence of shifts in demand.

Studies confirm that shifting from regulatory to price-based instruments can yield significant efficiency gains. In the United States, for example, a shift from standards-based regulation to permit trading for sulphur dioxide in the late 1990s was estimated to yield compliance cost savings of between USD 153 million to USD 358 million per year due to the flexibility it gave firms to respond to requirements to reduce emissions (Anthoff and Hahn, 2010).

That said, well-designed regulation can deliver strong net benefits and may be preferred by firms and other stakeholders in the policy process, even where prices are a technically superior alternative. Regulatory approaches may simply be more feasible in jurisdictions where constituencies are strongly against tax increases. This is important to the extent that large scale changes to production in sectors like energy may require significant prices increases which are politically unsustainable. In this regard, it is essential that policy options are subject to careful consultation with the private sector and civil society.

The regulatory environment also needs to be conducive to voluntary private sector initiatives. A case in point is the conditions needed to support payments for ecosystem services (PES); where the user or beneficiary of an ecosystem service makes a direct payment to an individual or community whose land use decisions have an impact on the ecosystem service provision. Such schemes currently tend to be dependent on government regulation as a service purchaser or in some intermediary role (Bumbudsanpharoke, 2010). They often hinge on the existence of secure land tenure and title.[8]

Regulatory conditions also need to provide sufficient flexibility to take advantage of the benefits of voluntary approaches from the private sector. Indeed, voluntary approaches have a useful complementary role to play within a green growth policy mix. In recent decades voluntary non-governmental initiatives, often involving business, have contributed much to measurement protocols for valuing environmental assets, gauging environmental and social impacts of investment, and life-cycle resource use and pollutant intensity. Increased commercial use of rating and eco-labelling can supplement other initiatives and policies to provide information about the environmental impact of products or available clean goods or activities. Voluntary approaches are not, however, without complications. They also cannot be relied upon to overcome fundamental market failures.[9]

Improving competition through, for example, reforming product market regulations is important for green growth. This is true for growth in general but is crucial for greening growth because competition is often least robust in network industries which have large environmental impacts (the electricity sector) or control strategic environmental services (such as water). Appropriate pro-competitive regulation which ensures wide access to networks by competing providers would help facilitate green growth. Competition facilitates more efficient resource use and, in conjunction with price instruments, leads to innovation.[10]

In some cases, the greening of growth may be constrained by barriers to competition or regulatory hurdles arise which were not previously apparent. For example, network regulations in most countries with competition in electricity generation have been designed without intermittent renewable energy generation in mind. Market rules can have the effect of excluding or adding unnecessary costs to the provision of intermittent power. Bidding systems which are conducted on a day-ahead basis effectively exclude wind power, for instance.[11] Such regulations may need to be changed in order to allow broad penetration of renewable generation in a competitive market system, while maintaining safe, stable and reliable networks.

Policy reform for improving competition also requires attention to environmental regulation which protects incumbent firms. Many environmental regulations impose more stringent requirements on entrants than incumbents, discouraging both firm entry and exit. These sorts of preferences, while they can be useful for facilitating the passage of environmental measures, have negative impacts on both environmental quality and productivity growth. Even some market-based instruments can have adverse impacts on entry and exit. For instance, when emission permits are given to incumbents for free, the question arises of how to allocate permits to new entrants (new-built installations) or to firms that plan to extend the capacity of existing installations. [12] Emission permits should be treated just like any other asset, *i.e.* they should not lose their value once a firm closes down. Conversely, new entrants and firms extending their capacity should not be rewarded by free permit allocation, as this would be tantamount to an entry subsidy.

Regulations governing trade and foreign direct investment (FDI) are also important as openness to trade and FDI can boost growth and make it greener at the same time.[13] Numerous tariff and non-tariff barriers remain in place around the world inhibiting the free flow of environmental goods (Steenblik and Kim, 2009). In addition, in some developing and emerging economies, high import tariffs on energy-consuming goods, like air conditioners and refrigerators, are also combining with subsidised electricity prices to encourage consumers to favour appliances that are cheap to buy but relatively inefficient to operate.[14] In the case of FDI, although the research is not unanimous, the weight of evidence indicates that inward FDI in developing countries is almost always at least as environmentally sensitive as domestic investment, and in most cases superior, sometimes substantially.[15]

A government's regulatory policy framework, including requirements for regulatory impact assessments (RIA), also has important influence on policy coherence by preventing the passage of regulations which are conducive to environmental harm. Research reveals that the *ex ante* analyses of regulatory initiatives, incorporating cost benefit analysis and an assessment of environmental impacts remain under-utilised (OECD, 2009a). This creates the potential for thwarting growth through unnecessary red tape, ineffective policy choices or unnecessarily costly regulatory initiatives.

RIA can, in general, make transparent any trade-offs in the comparison of alternative regulatory proposals, ensuring that appropriate weight is given to environmental aspects. Environmental regulations, while typically introducing costs of compliance for firms, can produce public benefits far in excess of these costs. However, standard methodologies may not always suffice in accounting for intangible environmental values and quantifying expected policy benefits (Box 2.3).

These are important dimensions of policy for green growth and greater attention should be paid to them in regulatory analysis. Useful approaches to dealing with these have been adopted in the United

States where an interagency group has established a consistent framework for the evaluation of benefits from reduced CO_2 emissions (also called social cost of carbon (SCC)). In the United Kingdom all impact assessments for new policy across government capture the absolute level of carbon emissions generated (in both the traded and non-traded sector), as well as a number of other environmental costs and benefits.

Information on the value and quality of many natural assets is limited. Measuring the contribution of ecosystems to societal well-being and economic growth would be a valuable way to improve regulatory decisions and integrating ecosystem services into economic policy. The United Kingdom has, for example, embarked on an ambitious National Ecosystem Assessment to assess how terrestrial, freshwater and marine ecosystems across the country have changed in the past and how they might continue to change in the future. The Assessment will help to quantify the state and value of the natural environment and the services it provides to society. It will assess policy and management options to ensure the integrity of natural systems in the future, and help raise awareness of their central importance to human well-being and economic prosperity.

Box 2.3.   Accounting for uncertainty and long-term impacts

The standard arithmetic for regulatory cost benefit analysis changes when systemic environmental risks are taken into account. This is because the nature of environmental impacts is uncertain and potentially irreversible. Long time frames involved mean standard time-accounting techniques (i.e. discounting) are inappropriate (OECD, 2006b).

The presence of uncertainty in conjunction with irreversibility changes the calculus of trade-offs because of the value in waiting to act until more information is available. That value increases significantly in the face of irreversibility. Examples of irreversibility include: the extraction of groundwater; oil spills and loss of some local ecosystem functions and biodiversity; bio-accumulative health impacts associated with water pollution; overfishing and commercial extinction of a fish stock; and large-scale deglaciation (OECD, 2008).

The value of the option to wait can be such that it dominates all other policy considerations. It does, however, operate along multiple dimensions depending on the nature of the issue at stake. On the one hand if, for example, there is uncertainty about the irreversible effects on biodiversity and ecosystem services from clear-felling old-growth forest then there is value in delaying exploitation of the resource until more information is available. When the magnitude of effects are potentially large and irreversible, such as in the case of deglaciation of the West Antarctic Ice Shelf due to climate change, there can be large (sunk) benefits from acting now to reduce greenhouse gas emissions and the risk of catastrophic change instead of waiting until the effects become clear and realising that nothing can be done about it (a feature of stock pollutants like greenhouse gases) (Pindyck, 2007; Weitzman, 2009). On the other hand, where there are sunk costs associated with investing in pollution abatement and pollutants are of the flow variety (such as particulate matter automotive emissions) there will be value in waiting until new abatement technologies become available. There would, however, be an important relationship between abatement policy and the invention of new abatement technologies which would need to be accounted for.

When evaluating impacts extending over long periods, it is necessary to express the costs of inaction borne far in the future in a manner which is commensurable with costs borne today. This implies adding a discount rate to future impacts or returns. The choice of the discount rate has a big impact on project or policy evaluation. In the face of uncertainty concerning future interest rates and the future path of the economy, a discount rate which declines through time may be appropriate (Weitzman, 2001; CGP, 2005). Depending on the degree of uncertainty involved, this value may converge on a low discount rate. It is also the case that "different discount rates should be used for different types of assets and services, factoring in their nature as public goods or private assets, and also whether they are capable of being manufactured or not (i.e. social discount rates for public goods and natural assets versus market discount rates for private goods and manufactured assets)" (Hepburn, 2007; TEEB, 2010). In the case of climate change, other issues than choice of discount rate will dominate any cost-benefit analysis, notably the presence of deep structural uncertainty and potentially unlimited exposure to damages (Weitzman, 2009).[16]

Enabling changes in consumer behaviour

Pricing the use of environmental resources has proven to be a powerful tool for influencing consumer and household decisions. For example, recent work based on a survey of 10 000 households across ten OECD countries indicates that households charged for water consume approximately 20% less water than those who are not (OECD, 2011d). In addition, households which are subject to unit pricing are more likely to install water-efficient and energy-efficient equipment at home (Figure 2.5). Similarly, fuel costs have a negative effect on car use and waste charges increase recycling volumes and encourage waste prevention.

However, behavioural studies indicate that consumers often focus on short-term costs, without fully considering longer-term factors. This suggests that efforts to highlight cost implications of consumer choices over the product life cycle may be needed to influence choices for consumer durables. Measures, for example, that encourage consumers to consider the savings that an energy efficient washer would achieve over time, compared to a lower priced model, could result in a shift in demand towards the "greener" product.

Figure 2.5.   Unit pricing and investment in conservation measures

As a percentage of households having invested in last 10 years

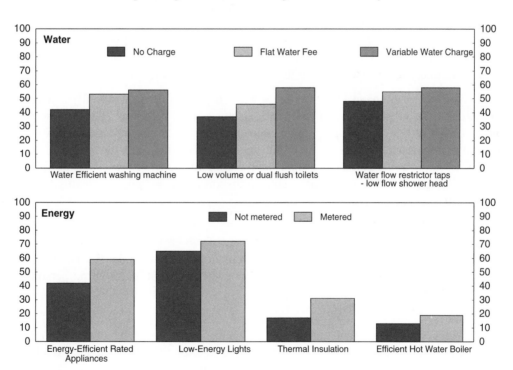

Source: OECD (2011), *Greening Household Behaviour: The Role of Public Policy.*

StatLink ⟶ http://dx.doi.org/10.1787/888932422154

While economic instruments are powerful tools, recent research suggests that "softer" instruments need to be given close attention in developing more comprehensive strategies for influencing consumer and household behaviour. Access to comprehensible and trustworthy information is central to strengthening markets for environmentally friendly products, particularly for goods and services where environmental attributes are less "visible". The manner in which information is presented and the way that choices are framed can influence consumer decisions. For example, individuals are seen as being more likely to respond to eco-labels if the environmental benefits co-exist with more direct personal benefits for the consumer, such as a reduced energy bills resulting from energy-saving behaviour (OECD, 2010g; 2010h; 2011d).

In response to growing consumer concern about environmental degradation and climate change, firms are expanding the use of "self-declared" claims as a corporate marketing tool (OECD, 2010g). Some of the claims, however, are general, while others are not well-defined. The scepticism and confusion that can result can diminish the value and effectiveness of green claims to consumers, thereby, undermining efforts to strengthen markets for green products. To be effective, claims therefore need to be clear, well-defined, substantiated and properly monitored through the development of environmental claims guides, standards and codes (OECD, 2010g; 2010i). This can generally be achieved under advertising laws that allow authorities to move against such claims (ICPEN, 2010).

Third party certification (OECD, 2010h) can also improve consumer confidence in the environmental attributes of products. Governments have been active on this front, as in the United States "Energy Star" programme and Germany's "Blue Angel" initiative. Governments can further address information issues by providing consumers with comparative information themselves, or by encouraging firms to do so, mandatorily or on a voluntary basis. This can help consumers reduce their search costs by making it easier for them to compare products.[17]

In addition, many markets in which household consumption patterns are particularly environmentally-sensitive are subject to important secondary market failures and barriers. In such cases, it can be efficient for policy makers to introduce complementary policy measures when market barriers and failures discourage particular investments. For instance, the benefits of investing in insulation or efficient boilers are likely to be much less for tenants than owner- occupiers.

Moreover, many choices made by households with respect to environmentally-sensitive goods are undertaken against a backdrop in which the public sector plays an important role, whether as service provider or regulator. While encouraging household demand for environmental quality through prices and information is important, the role of the public sector in affecting the supply of environment-related public services to households can be an important complement. Measures such as the provision of collection services for recyclable materials, public transportation, or "green" electricity supply clearly matter (OECD, 2011e).

Non-economic factors can be important in changing consumer behaviour. Education can play an important role in forming attitudes to environmental issues from early childhood on, and actions to raise awareness are fundamental in changing consumer behaviour. Research in the United Kingdom, for example, indicates that the behaviour of others influences people; that learning the personal benefits of taking action to support sustainable consumption is very important; and that a sense of making a difference matters (OECD 2009b; 2010h; 2010g).

Empirical evidence indicates that consumers and households could be more motivated to reduce energy consumption when their performance is measured against their neighbours, than they would by more general information describing the environmental harm caused by excessive energy consumption (Houde and Todd, 2010). In addition, the OECD's household survey shows that other variables, such as a more general sense of civic duty (rather than just specific concern for environmental issues) can be important in, for example, explaining support for recycling programmes (OECD, 2011d). In some cases, however, consumers are unresponsive to price changes because of a lack of affordable alternatives.

Innovation

The core of transforming an economy is innovation. Innovation and the resulting creative destruction mean new ideas, new entrepreneurs and new business models. It contributes to the establishment of new markets, leads to the creation of new jobs and is a key ingredient of any effort to improve people's quality of life.

Innovation today is as much about firms and organisations finding new ways of doing things or ways to use novel technologies as about breakthroughs that occur in the lab. Technological breakthroughs and their diffusion in the market are of course extremely important, but so too are the organisational and systemic changes that need to accompany them. For example, green innovation aimed at transport systems and cities will involve major organisational and institutional changes. Technologies are often only effective in enhancing performance when accompanied by complementary investments, *e.g.* in skills (OECD, 2004).

Without innovation, it will be very difficult and very costly to address major environmental issues. Assessments of the cost of climate mitigation, for example, suggest that if two carbon-free renewable technologies in the electricity and non-electricity sectors can be made competitive,[18] then mitigation costs in 2050 would be halved – from about 4% of world GDP to under 2% – compared with a scenario without such technologies. Innovation is therefore crucial in enabling green and growth to go hand in hand.

The beauty of innovation is that, for the most part, it is a positive-sum game where the gains of one country do not need to come at the cost of another. This makes the diffusion of new ideas or technologies generally as important as the inventions behind them. Innovations need to be taken up as widely as possible for shared prosperity and to reduce the costs of addressing environmental risks, especially those from which we all gain from collective action such as climate change.

On the supply-side, many of the enabling conditions for innovation are the same whether one is concerned with green innovation or innovation more generally. The fundamental drivers and barriers are similar, as confirmed by empirical work at the OECD which found that green innovation thrives in a sound environment for overall innovation. However, the rate and pattern of "green" innovation is also heavily influenced by other factors, notably the environmental policy framework. As discussed in the OECD Innovation Strategy (OECD, 2010j), a number of framework policies for innovation are important.

A policy environment based on core "framework conditions" – sound macroeconomic policy, competition, openness to international trade and investment, tax and financial systems – is also a fundamental building block of any effective (green) growth strategy and allows innovation to thrive.

Firms are essential for translating good ideas into jobs and wealth, and require good and stable framework conditions. Large firms are important as they possess the scale, scope and experience to commercialise and diffuse new products and technologies at a global scale. New innovative firms are also important as they often exploit opportunities that have been neglected by more established companies. Many regulatory systems impose more stringent abatement requirements on entrants, discouraging both entry and exit, thus inadvertently slowing the rate of innovation (OECD, 2010j). Small and medium-sized enterprises (SME) account for the bulk of all firms, but they often face challenges in the later stage of the innovation chain, specifically in financing and getting products to market, and often have weaker capabilities for innovation than large firms. Policy can help to improve their access to finance and information, foster their participation in knowledge networks, and support the development of skills.

Access to finance is one of the key constraints for business-led innovation, which is inherently risky and may require a long-term horizon. As the financial system has a central role in fostering green innovation, restoring its health should be a priority. Well-functioning venture capital markets and the securitisation of innovation-related assets (*e.g.* intellectual property) are key sources of finance for many innovative start-ups and need to be developed further. When public funds are deployed, they should be channelled through existing market-based systems, and shaped with a clear market approach.

Labour market policies need to be flexible enough to facilitate the movement of workers and resources from declining to innovative firms. Too much rigidity in labour markets has been shown to reduce innovation for a given level of R&D (Cotis, de Serres and Duval, 2010). Having the right people is also important and requires relevant education as well as the development of skills to complement formal education.

Governments play an important role in investing in research, in particular in basic research, and in fostering an efficient knowledge infrastructure, for example broadband networks, which needs to be combined with regulatory frameworks that support access and competition. Moreover, adequate and effective protection and enforcement of intellectual property rights are key to providing incentives to innovation and the diffusion of knowledge.

Green innovation

Green technology development *is* accelerating in some areas. The number of patented inventions in renewable energy (+24%), electric and hybrid vehicles (+20%), and energy efficiency in building and lighting (+11%) increased more rapidly than total patents (+6%) between 1999 and 2008. Most of the green technology development is concentrated in a relatively small number of countries and there is a considerable specialisation across countries. For selected climate mitigation technologies, Japan's patent applications in 2008, for example, were relatively more concentrated in innovation related to energy-efficient buildings and lighting, as well as electric and hybrid vehicles, while the United States was particularly prominent in the area of renewable energy (Figure 2.6).

Figure 2.6.   Patenting in climate change mitigation technologies

Patent applications at the Patent Co-operation Treaty (PCT), number in 2008

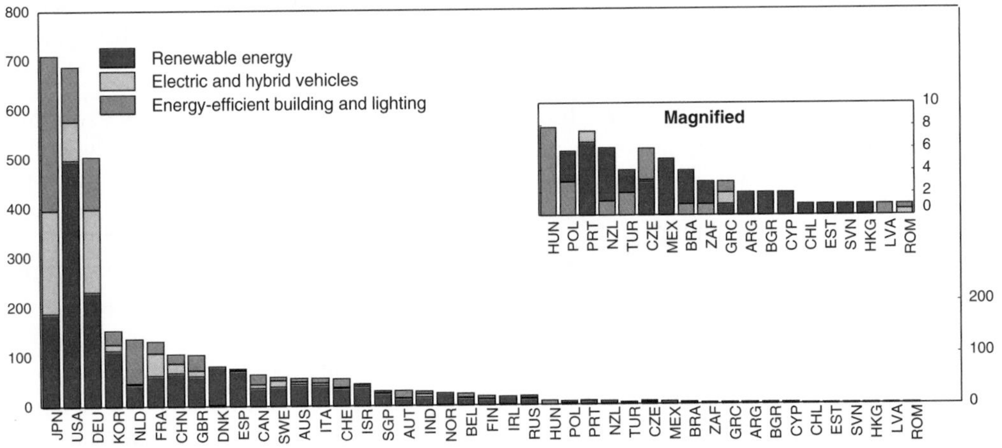

Note: Information on data for Cyprus: see endnotes 19 and 20. Information on data for Israel: see endnote 21.

Source: OECD Patent Database, January 2011.

StatLink ⬛ http://dx.doi.org/10.1787/888932422173

While some data are available on green technologies, much less information is available on the related non-technological changes and innovation, such as in the introduction of new business models, work patterns, city planning or transportation arrangements, that will also be instrumental in driving green growth. There is some evidence that the scope of green innovation is broadening, however. For example, manufacturing firms have moved from end-of-pipe solutions to approaches that minimise material and energy flows by changing products and production methods and reusing waste as a new resource for production (OECD, 2010k). Advances are also being made through better management practices and integrated strategies that are contributing to a range of new business models (OECD, 2011e).

Innovation with an environmental or "green" flavour faces additional barriers which exacerbate existing ones. When firms and households do not have to pay for environmental services or the costs of pollution, the demand for green innovation is constrained and there are fewer incentives for companies to invest in innovation.

Boosting green innovation therefore benefits from clear and stable market signals, *e.g.* carbon pricing or other market instruments addressing the externalities associated with environmental challenges. Such signals will enhance the incentives for firms to adopt and develop green innovations, and help to indicate the commitment of governments to move towards greener growth. They will also enhance efficiency in allocating resources by establishing markets for green innovation, and will lower the costs of addressing environmental challenges. Taxes and other pricing instruments are included in Japan's recent "New Growth Strategy".

Recent experiences suggest that carbon pricing contributes primarily to incremental rather than disruptive innovation, however. This tends to increase efficiency but may also lead to growing consumption, as has been the case in personal transport. Given the other market failures that green innovation is facing, complementary policies are needed.

A key question in this context is: how and where governments should focus their efforts. In terms of how, there are three key ways that governments can lend their support to green innovation. One is in funding relevant research, whether public or private. Energy and environmental R&D, for example, account for a very small share of GDP relative to their centrality to economic life (Figure 2.7).

Figure 2.7.   Public spending in energy- and environment-related R&D

OECD average

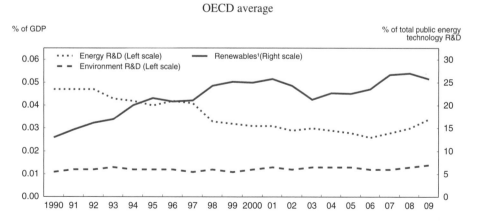

1. Energy technology R&D expenditures directed towards "Renewable energy" and "Energy efficiency" measures.

Source: Energy and environment R&D as a % of GDP based on OECD (2011), Research and Development Statistics Database and Renewables as % of total Energy R&D from IEA (2011), RD&D Budget Database, covering the 28 IEA member countries.

StatLink ᔑᗕ *http://dx.doi.org/10.1787/888932422192*

Another way to support green innovation is to target barriers to its early-stage commercial development. Access to finance is especially difficult for firms engaged in green innovation, due to the relative immaturity of the market, and thus greater perceived commercial risk. While, markets are likely to price this risk more accurately as markets mature (OECD, 2011f), this may take time.

A third way to strengthen green innovation is to use demand-side innovation policies. Standards, well-designed regulations and public procurement, for example, can encourage green innovation in markets where price signals alone are not fully effective. For instance, following the introduction of the German packaging ordinance in 1989, there was a take-off of patents of biodegradable packaging (OECD, 2010l). These three approaches are further elaborated below.

Strengthening research and development

Investment in basic and long-term research underpins much of the innovation process and provides the foundation for future innovation. Such research has a long time horizon and often has no immediate commercial applications, which implies it is unlikely to be undertaken by the private sector. It can help address fundamental scientific challenges and help foster technologies that are considered too risky, uncertain or long-gestating for the private sector.

Some studies have argued for large investments in relevant public research along the lines of the Apollo moon project, which involved large public investments in research. However, unlike this project, green innovations will need to be applied throughout the economy, and mostly in the private sector. Driving down the costs of new green technologies is often key to its uptake and diffusion in the market (Box 2.4).

Box 2.4.   Fostering a green revolution – the experience from ICT

If green innovation is to lead to a substantial acceleration in economic growth and the creation of new firms, jobs and industries, green technologies and innovation will need to become widespread throughout society. One recent example of this process is the rapid diffusion of ICT over the past decades, which is typically regarded as having led to a new technological revolution, contributing to productivity and employment growth. The example of this technology may prove instructive in better understanding the possible impacts of green technologies on the economy, and the conditions under which technologies become effective in substantially enhancing economic performance. A few elements from the experience with ICT may be particularly relevant for the current debate:

- First, one major factor in the strong growth resulting from ICT was (and remains) the rapid decline in the real price of information and communications technologies. The US producer price index for electronic computer manufacturing, for example, fell by about 14% annually between January 1991 and January 2011. This rapid price decline enabled ICT to be applied across the economy, at very low costs, which subsequently contributed to improvements in performance across the economy. Green technologies have not yet experienced such a massive price decline and their future impact will rely in part on the extent to which prices can be brought down.

- Second, the experience with ICT suggests that much of the impacts and job creation resulting from new technology are not in the production or manufacturing of the technology, but in its application throughout the economy. While some countries benefitted from having an ICT-producing sector, most gained from ICT through its application throughout the economy, notably in the services sector. If this experience provides any guidance for a possible green revolution, it suggests that growth will result more from the application and diffusion of green technologies, including the associated services, than from the production of the technology, which tends to be highly concentrated.

- Third, the impacts of ICT were heavily dependent on complementary changes in work practices, skills and organisations, which in turn rely heavily on the flexibility of labour and product markets. If this provides any guidance to the current context, it suggests that green innovation is more likely to have positive impacts in economies that have well-functioning product and labour markets.

- Fourth, the experience with ICT also suggests that the ultimate applications and uses of technologies are virtually impossible to predict, as are the areas of growth and decline. Only some of the firms that started the ICT revolution are still successful firms today, and many new firms, applications and business models have emerged over the past decades, many in areas that were not predicted only a few years ago. This includes a wide range of applications in green innovation.

To further complicate matters, research that yields innovation in a particular sector can come from areas of research that are not obvious (Igami and Saka, 2007). For example, a mapping of scientific fields that influence innovation in green technologies, as measured by patenting, shows that chemistry and material sciences are at least as important as research on energy and the environment (Figure 2.8).

Figure 2.8.   The innovation-science link in selected green technologies

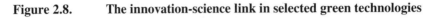

Patent-science link via citations, 2000-07

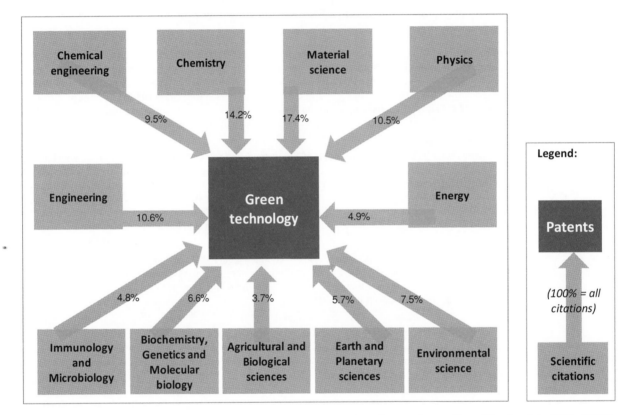

Source: OECD (2010), *Measuring Innovation – A New Perspective*, based on Scopus Custom Data, Elsevier, July 2009; OECD, Patent Database, January 2010; and EPO, Worldwide Patent Statistical Database, September 2009.

This finding is important as it relates to spending decisions. While government spending on energy and environmental R&D have not kept pace with the growing urgency of environmental challenges, this do not necessarily imply that more investment is needed in these areas alone. Much transformative innovation results from spill-over effects from other sectors, as demonstrated by the impacts of ICT on the transport and energy sectors.

Encouraging the development of more generic or general purpose technologies, such as materials technologies, nanotechnologies, biotechnologies, green chemistry and ICT, is therefore just as important as spending on energy or environmental R&D (OECD, 2011e). Moreover, addressing the complex research challenges increasingly requires approaches that involve multi-disciplinary and interdisciplinary funding, rather than funding along scientific disciplines. Social sciences will also play an important role; for example, understanding consumer behaviour will be important to develop effective approaches to changing consumption patterns. Advanced management practices (*e.g.* environmental accounting) can also result in improved environmental performance (Johnstone, 2007).

Some public investments in research should be channelled to specific areas, *e.g.* through mission-oriented programmes in areas where research can resolve known challenges. For example, IEA analysis of the investment in energy R&D needed to deliver low-carbon growth suggests that a substantial global gap exists between required and current R&D expenditure in certain fields (IEA, 2010b). However, exploratory research focused on potentially radical innovations - characterised by high risk and uncertainty - should also be included in the funding mix, although it will only deliver results in the long run.

Given the significant potential for research and innovation to reduce the costs of meeting environmental goals, governments should increase their public investment in relevant research. However, this may also involve providing greater direction to existing research budgets, *e.g.* in prioritising thematic and mission-oriented research programmes aimed at addressing these challenges. Moreover, increased funding will only be effective in strengthening green innovation if the links between science and business are well established; in many countries, this still requires policy action.

There is also a question on how to focus national efforts. Few countries have the scale or capabilities to engage in every area of research that could contribute to green growth. Governments should typically focus their efforts on areas where their research system has a strong capability or where there is a need to develop or adapt technologies to their own needs and circumstances. At the same time, international competition is essential to drive down the costs of green innovation.

Supporting innovation and deployment

Investing in relevant research is only one approach towards green innovation. Another way is to address specific barriers and market failures to green innovation. Such barriers include the relative immaturity of the market for green innovation, as well as the dominance of existing designs in energy and transport markets, which can create entry barriers for new technologies due to, for example, the high fixed costs of developing new infrastructures. In particular, when projects face high technology risks and are capital intensive, they are very hard to fund with either project or debt financing or venture capital and can fall into a funding *"Valley of Death"*.

Where governments should direct their support is a difficult issue to grapple with. In picking where support should go there is always a risk of promoting activities that may have occurred anyway. Similarly, there is a risk that more appropriate technologies or practices will emerge that should have been supported but policy has locked the economy into a less desirable pathway. On the other hand, too little support can preclude the achievement of environmental objectives. In many cases, such as driving low-carbon growth or decarbonising energy systems, large scale system-wide changes need to happen in a relatively short space of time. This presents both costs to the environment and potentially costs to growth.

This commends a portfolio of public investment where funding approaches need to be tailored to the different stages of technology development. Government funding is most relevant for early-stage technology development, while private finance tends to assume a larger share of later-stage technology deployment and commercialisation. The case for government action differs according to the key stages of the innovation cycle (IEA, 2010b):

1. For promising but not yet mature technologies: at this stage, government will need to support research and large-scale demonstration and begin to assess infrastructure and regulatory needs.

2. For technologies that are technically proven, but require additional financial support: in this case, government may wish to provide incentives (*e.g.* feed-in tariffs) to create a market, combined with regulatory frameworks/standards.

3. For technologies that are close to competitive today: governments can provide technology-neutral incentives that are removed upon achievement of market competitiveness.

4. For technologies that are competitive today: governments play a role in building public acceptance/adoption by identifying and addressing market and informational barriers.

In general, policies for innovation and deployment need to encourage experimentation to bring about new options that can help strengthen environmental performance at the lowest cost. This should involve a vigorous process of national and global competition among alternative technologies and innovations, to bring about those options that have the best performance. Governments should level the playing field between alternative options, but should in general avoid supporting specific technologies and solutions over others, emphasising competition and technology neutrality.

However, such policies may not always be enough, as green innovation faces additional barriers in some markets, *e.g.* barriers to entry in the electricity sector. In practice, many governments therefore provide targeted support for specific technology fields. As noted above, provision of such support can be risky because of the lack of information on the maturity of specific technologies, and their likely future commercial potential. The design of government policy is therefore essential, as further discussed below.

The case of renewable energy is instructive. Denmark's experience with feed-in-tariffs (FITs)[22] in stimulating the wind power industry between the mid-1980s and the late 1990s is often cited as an example. The Danish government guaranteed a relatively high internal rate of return, which provided a strong incentive for investment in wind power. In 1990, the capacity of installed onshore wind power in the country amounted already to 343 MW, 76% of the total capacity installed in Western Europe. This stable and sizable home market provided the Danish wind industry with the necessary testing ground for their technologies. Once a certain level of technical maturity had been achieved within the domestic market, Danish companies moved to the global market (Lewis and Wiser, 2007). However, Denmark's success with FITs has not been repeated widely.

In the case of Germany's Renewable Energy Sources Act (2000), FITs were implemented with a view toward encouraging innovation across a diverse portfolio of renewable energy sources. FITs were differentiated according to perceived maturity, with the rates declining over time to reflect shifts along the learning curve, and to maintain the diversity of the portfolio. While the "predictability" of the rates was seen as being essential, there have been periodic revisions to reflect changing economic conditions (Lipp, 2007).

In some cases, other instruments may be more promising than feed-in-tariffs as they are focused on performance rather than specific technologies. For example, renewable energy certificates, that include requirements on the percentage of electricity that must be generated by renewable sources, give more broad-based incentives to innovation in alternative energy than FITs (Johnstone, Haščič, and Popp, 2010). However, such measures are unlikely to have a significant impact on less mature technologies since investors will focus on those areas which are "closer to market".

Providing support for more "radical" innovations in a manner which is not excessively prescriptive is a significant policy challenge. Technology prizes have a role to play in certain areas, as they reward the achievement of a specific goal (Newell and Wilson, 2005). Directing investment to enabling technologies will also help address problems associated with providing targeted support to specific technologies. OECD analysis shows that a boost in public funding of renewable energy R&D would be more "productive" if it was allocated to enabling technologies such as energy storage or grid management, rather than to specific generating technologies (*e.g.* wind, ocean, solar) (Johnstone and Haščič, 2011).

While policies to support specific green technologies may be needed to overcome barriers to commercialisation, the design of such policies is essential to avoid capture by vested interests and ensure that they are efficient in meeting public policy objectives. Focusing policies on performance rather than specific technologies or cost recovery is essential. Other important elements of good design include independence of the agencies making funding decisions, use of peer review and competitive procedures with clear criteria for project selection. Support for commercialisation should also be temporary and accompanied by clear sunset clauses and transparent phase-out schedules. As noted before, support policies also require a good understanding of the state of development of green technologies; support for commercialisation should not be provided before technologies reach a sufficiently mature state.

Small and medium-sized enterprises (SMEs) face additional problems in adopting green innovations, as they often have weak innovation capabilities. Policy can help to improve access to finance, enable small and medium-sized enterprises to participate in knowledge networks, strengthen the skills that can lead to innovation, and reduce the regulatory burden on firms. Opening (green) public procurement to SMEs may also help in strengthening green innovation in such firms, and is the objective of programmes such as the United States Small Business Innovation Research programme.

Demand-side policies

Demand-side instruments, such as public procurement, can help foster markets for new products and services, for example through demonstration effects, and counter gaps in the supply of finance at the early stages. They can also help accelerate the emergence of technologies for which there is an urgent time-bound societal need and that are subject to specific barriers, such as network effects and market dominance. One example is the electric car, where public procurement could potentially play a role in strengthening market acceptance and boosting the development of the necessary network. Public procurement also plays an important role in the greening of governments. As with direct support, governments should generally ensure that their procurement policies are technology neutral and focused on performance.

Demand-side policies often imply a lead role for the public sector. However, the public sector is not always best placed to support the innovation process, and new capacities may need to be developed. For instance, as regards public procurement, the traditional focus on cost alone as well as the problem of fragmentation of public demand (often between different levels of government) can limit potential scale effects for innovative procurement. Furthermore, environmental goals must be balanced against the need for competition, transparency and accountability in public procurement. OECD countries should adhere to national competition and public procurement rules as well as related international standards and obligations (*e.g.* the WTO Government Procurement Agreement).

Standards play an important role for green innovation, in particular in network industries, in that they can facilitate a critical mass of users. Developing a common set of well-designed specifications, such as on the interoperability of smart grids and on connections between electric vehicles and the charging infrastructure, supports market development and stimulates private investment by avoiding the emergence of different technology formats. For example, the National Institute of Standards and Technology (NIST), an agency of the United States Commerce Department, co-ordinates a Smart Grid

Interoperability Standards Project with the aim to identify and develop standards critical to achieving a reliable and robust smart grid. The setting of standards is mainly the responsibility of industry bodies, although the government often acts as facilitator or co-ordinator. If standardisation is introduced too early, it could shut out better technologies. But if standardisation occurs too late, then the costs of transition to the new standard could be high enough to slow or prevent diffusion.

Regulation can be regarded as another tool to spur innovation. For example, the Promotion of Renewable Energies Heat Act (2009) in Germany stipulates that owners of newly-constructed buildings must use renewable energies. Moreover, building owners who use particularly efficient innovative technologies, or that have low emissions figures, will receive public support. The impact of regulation on innovation is not straightforward *a priori*, however, and often depends on specific characteristics of the market. The design of regulations is also important; they should be sufficiently stringent to encourage innovation; stable enough to give investors confidence; flexible enough to foster genuinely novel solutions; be closely targeted on the policy goal; and provide incentives for continuous innovation. Regulations can play this role in certain markets, but are typically a second-best solution to market-based instruments.

Technology transfer and diffusion

Ensuring a wide diffusion of green technologies will be as important as their invention, in particular in addressing global environmental issues. The speed of deployment of, for example, existing low-carbon technologies will partly determine the global costs of climate-change mitigation and adaptation.

International transfers of green technology occur primarily between developed countries (Table 2.3). Recent data, however, indicate that transfers in green technologies from OECD to non-OECD countries have been increasing over the last years. China alone accounts for three-quarters of the climate-mitigation transfers from OECD to non-OECD countries. There is also significant potential for North-South green technology transfers, as well as for South-South exchanges, particularly since these countries may have developed inventions that are better tailored to the needs of developing countries (Dechezleprêtre *et al.*, 2011).

Table 2.3.   Distribution of exported climate-mitigation inventions

2000-2005

Origin \ Destination	OECD	Non-OECD
OECD	73% (77%)	22% (16%)
Non-OECD	4% (6%)	1% (1%)

Note: Measured using patent data by origin of inventor and destination in which patent protection is sought. As a benchmark the total flows for technology transfers are displayed in parentheses.

Source: Dechezlepretre *et al.* (2011) "Invention and Transfer of Climate Change Mitigation Technologies: A Global Analysis" in *Review of Environmental Economics and Policy*, (forthcoming). Reprinted by permission from Oxford University Press, copyright 2011.

Adoption of sound environmental policy plays an important role in driving international technology diffusion, as it contributes to the creation of markets for eco-innovations and provides firms with the incentives to acquire new technologies. Indeed, industrialised countries with more advanced environmental regulations have attracted more technology transfer.

However, the lack of strict environmental policy in developing countries is not the only explanation for the lower rates of environmental technology transfer to these countries as there is a similar pattern of low diffusion for all technologies. More general factors such as lack of financial resources, openness to trade and foreign direct investment, the quality of the IPR system and local capacities (*e.g.* human capital) also help to explain why technology diffusion is concentrated in developed countries.

Since technology transfers take place through market channels such as trade, FDI or licensing, they occur more frequently in open economies. Numerous tariff and non-tariff barriers to trade in green technologies remain in place, however, which inhibit their free flow (Steenblik and Kim, 2009). In some developing and emerging economies, high import tariffs on energy-consuming goods, like air conditioners and refrigerators, combine with subsidised electricity prices to encourage consumers to favour appliances that are relatively inefficient to operate.

Lowering barriers to trade in services is also important. Deployment of climate-change mitigation and adaptation technologies often depend on the availability of specialised services, including those imported from other countries, notably business services, construction, environmental and energy services. Foreign investment is also important and responds to a healthy business environment that includes adequate governance and economic institutions.

Tension can arise between technology diffusion and maintaining appropriate incentives for investment in innovation which is aggravated by the desirability of transferring clean technologies to emerging countries before they proceed to invest massively in potentially dirty technologies. IPRs provide an important incentive to invest in innovation by allowing firms to recover their investment costs.

IPRs should be well protected and appropriately enforced which implies that IPR regimes should be of high quality. Patent systems need to be properly designed to ensure that they provide strong incentives for innovation but also foster the public benefits that flow from dissemination of knowledge into the marketplace. Competition authorities play an important role in ensuring that patents are not used anti-competitively.

More generally, there is strong evidence that countries need absorptive capacities in order to successfully adopt foreign technology (Haščič and Johnstone, 2011). The higher the level of domestic human capital, the higher the level of technology transfer as well as the local spillovers from trade and FDI. This illustrates the importance of long-term education and capacity building policies in promoting technology transfer.

To accelerate the diffusion of innovation, new mechanisms that enhance technology transfer to developing countries are currently being developed *e.g.* voluntary patent pools and other collaborative mechanisms for leveraging IP (Maskus, 2010). Some good practice already exists but significant scale-up is required. Governments need to underpin such new mechanisms by supporting investments in the required knowledge networking infrastructure, fostering the sharing of public-sector knowledge, and developing guidance and soft rules to underpin these mechanisms.

To diffuse green technologies to the least-developed countries, multilateral action might also be considered to enhance access to green technologies for these countries. Experience in other areas, such as medicines for infectious diseases, shows this can work if it is well designed and the private sector is involved from the beginning. Enabling more systematically all countries and firms to build on the knowledge resulting from basic research undertaken by public institutes would also help.

Policy considerations

There is no single recipe to follow for driving green innovation. There is a diversity of possible approaches depending on the context (See *Tools for Delivering on Green Growth*: Table 7). This diversity commends special attention to governance arrangements around the policies to foster green innovation. In particular, this requires policies with a medium- and long-term perspective, and attention from policy makers at the highest level. Governance also involves co-ordination of simultaneous policy actions and consideration of possible interactions with policies with other objectives. Simply developing additional policies will not improve coherence; existing policies may have to be adjusted or phased out.

Yet, policies for green growth and innovation often remain compartmentalised in different departments and agencies, including at various geographical scales. This can create obstacles to co-operation and lead to a proliferation of duplicative and wasteful innovation policies. The budget process, as one of government's main decision-making tools, can help lead to effective innovation policies.

Policies to foster green innovation will benefit from continued evaluation and monitoring, to improve the effectiveness and efficiency of policies over time, and to take advantage of the development of new scientific insights and new technologies and innovations. The required policy changes resulting from evaluation will have to be balanced against the need for policy stability over time.

Policy also needs to consider the timing of innovations, as this may precipitate an advantage of one technology or innovation over another. For example, a technology having greater short-term advantages over another technology may become too dominant and "lock out" other technologies. Even if the long-term benefits of the "locked-in" technology would result in lower overall social benefits, it may succeed at the exclusion of other technologies. Moreover, if policy focuses exclusively on the deployment of currently available technologies, this will reduce the market for future innovations, which will reduce incentives to invest in R&D and efforts to develop such innovations. A related challenge, in particular in addressing climate change is whether to focus on accelerating the deployment of existing technologies or also support the development of new options for the future.

There are no simple answers to these questions, and policy will need to do both, accelerate the application of existing technologies, *e.g.* in strengthening energy efficiency, and develop new options for the future. One approach that can help inform long-term investment decisions associated with the introduction of new technologies and innovations involves the use of scenario studies, technology foresight and road mapping. This can provide insights into the scope for technological progress and innovation in different areas and may therefore help in guiding decisions.

Fostering a diverse range of potential options for action, and delaying some of the most lumpy and irreversible investments, may also help in preserving options for the deployment of new technologies and innovations as they emerge. This is one additional reason for a strong policy effort focusing on research, innovation and entrepreneurship, as these all contribute to the process of experimentation that underpins the emergence and development of new options. In addition, having a strong focus on policies to strengthen the market for green innovations, may also help in ensuring that policy does not get unduly locked into poor supply-side decisions.

Finally, green innovation is not only about new technologies. Non-technological innovation, including changes in cities and transport systems, as well as organisational and behavioural changes, will play an important role in accompanying the introduction of green technologies. Examples include the introduction of environmental management systems, or of new business models, such as energy-saving companies (OECD, 2010m). Governments should foster such innovation, and need to consider whether their framework policies are sufficiently conducive to such innovation, *e.g.* in addressing regulatory barriers in product markets that might limit the necessary structural change. Labour market policies are also important, as they help firms and workers adjust to change.

Investing in infrastructure

Shifting to a greener growth trajectory requires special attention to network infrastructure such as energy, transport, water and communications networks. There is considerable potential for infrastructure investment to contribute to economic growth and prosperity because it enables trade specialisation, competition, access to new resources, the diffusion of technology and new organisational practices (OECD, 2009c). Well planned infrastructure development can reduce water and air pollution and curb unsustainable land use change further enhancing development. Damage to infrastructure in the context of climate change can be limited if climatic changes are accounted for in the initial design, location and material selection.

Infrastructure is a large or high growth sector in much of the world, with the highest rates of growth occurring in the developing world. For many countries, especially those outside the OECD, there are opportunities to leap-frog by introducing greener and more efficient infrastructures, and to improve the climate resilience of infrastructures such as water supply facilities, roads and ports. Greening growth will require both investment in new infrastructure as well as better planned and managed infrastructure.

Energy

The energy sector poses a particular challenge in the context of green growth given the scale of change that this sector requires and the extent to which many countries are locked into polluting and GHG emitting energy sources in the near term.

Fossil fuels in particular will continue to dominate energy supply for some time simply because they are so energy dense – storing an enormous amount of energy by volume compared to other readily available energy sources – and because our societies and infrastructure have evolved around them. Also, innovation and change take time.[23] At the same time, new sources of energy need to be deployed on a scale equivalent to the industrial revolution. Without decisive action, energy-related emissions of CO_2 will double by 2050. Retrofitting these carbon-intensive systems could be very costly, so a range of measures need to be taken today to avoid locking-in such infrastructure.

Energy efficiency, many types of renewable energy, carbon capture and storage, low emission non-renewable energy sources, smart grids and new transport technologies could all contribute to curtailing greenhouse gas emissions while promoting energy security. This will also deliver wider environmental and social benefits (Figure 2.9).

Figure 2.9. **Energy technology pathways and mitigation**

Gt CO$_2$

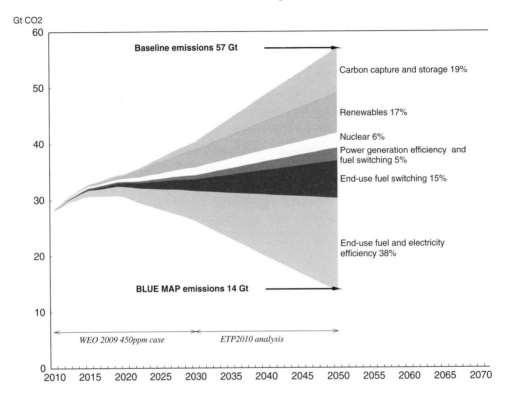

Source: IEA (2010), *Energy Technology Perspectives 2010.*

Forward-looking policies are needed to establish network infrastructure which is suitable for next generation technologies. This is especially so for energy infrastructure where the increased use of renewable energy introduces challenges for conventional infrastructure networks. Historically, electricity was typically produced centrally by large generating units, often powered by fossil fuels, and transported in one direction to customers who were able to consume as much as they liked at a single time-averaged retail price.

A variety of pressures are putting the traditional approach to electricity production and distribution under close scrutiny, including: *(a)* the need to accommodate a large amount of inherently intermittent renewable generating capacity; *(b)* the need to accommodate a large amount of small-scale, distributed energy generation and storage facilities such as roof-top solar installations, or plug-in electric vehicles; and *(c)* pressure to improve the utilisation of network resources by shifting consumption decisions over time, *e.g.* to off-peak periods.

In the past, *(a)* and *(b)* may have been met by simply building more network assets. However, increasing costs of construction, especially in congested areas, and public pressure on electricity bills has led to pressure to achieve smarter use of existing resources, through a cluster of innovations collectively known as the "smart grid". The smart grid depends on various information and communication technologies (ICTs) to increase efficiency, provide transparency to customers and utilities and equip the energy sector with solutions to structural challenges due to more integration of renewable energy sources and shift in electricity demand, for example from plug-in electric vehicles.

Many of these technologies already exist and have been in place for many years in the control of the high-voltage transmission network and the associated producers and consumers. The primary impact of the smart grid concept will be in the extension of these technologies to better link power from distributed generation to businesses and smaller consumers.

Other solutions to improving network efficiency include increased integration of networks across regions or countries. In Europe, for example, the efficiency of energy supply could be improved through enhanced regional interconnection. This kind of investment has large incremental paybacks due to network effects. Increased interconnection would permit wider distribution of renewable energy from its different sources. It also dramatically increases scope for demand management on the network where differences in time zones and climate give scope for demand smoothing thereby improving efficiency of generation and network use (ECF, 2010). Similar opportunities exist in North America where most grid infrastructure is regionalised.

Demand management has many potential efficiency benefits, especially in terms of shifting demand off-peak. An increase in demand responsiveness also significantly reduces the scope for the exercise of market power to which wholesale electricity markets tend to be prone.

Such transformation of the energy sector requires significant investments in developing and deploying smart grid solutions. However, energy sector business models have traditionally depended on volume sales and the sector has seen relatively low and falling R&D expenditures (private *and* public), as already discussed above. Government action can be decisive in addressing the two issues:

- Diversification towards sustainable energy sector products, services and infrastructures can be achieved through *i)* market mechanisms, *e.g.* increased transparency and easy access to information, *ii)* financial incentives, *e.g.* contribution to investment costs or tax breaks for infrastructure investments, *iii)* targeted regulation such as recent EU Directives mandating a roll-out of smarter electricity meters that, among other benefits, provide improved information to final customers (EU (2006) 2006/32/EC and EU (2009) 2009/72/EC).

- Innovation can result from higher R&D spending in the sector, but transformative solutions often come as "spill-overs" from adjacent industries and are increasingly based on multi-disciplinary research. Recent start-ups have developed new technologies and business models around solar power (Ausra), electricity billing data (Opower) and electric vehicles (Better Place). Most have gained significant attention from private investors and the public sector. Governments can put in place frameworks that support entrepreneurship and capital acquisition of such start-ups. They can also support cross-sector technology development and diffusion, and government agencies with energy, telecommunications and related portfolios should join forces in the development and use of technologies for energy and the environment.

Governments should be aware of potential bottlenecks and risks as electricity grids become smarter. Increased reliance on communication networks can test existing infrastructures regarding speed, quality of service, security, reliability and equal treatment of competitors' information. Privacy issues around access to individual customers' data need to be addressed in co-ordination with user associations, consumer protection and law enforcement agencies, and other stakeholders.

The defining characteristics of the energy sector in many developing countries include low access to modern energy sources, 1.6 billion people still lack access to electricity, coupled with significant local environmental impacts arising from the use of traditional fuels. For instance, traditional cooking and heating facilities (*e.g.* burning of biomass or coal) used by more than half the world's population are significant sources of indoor pollution, especially in poorly ventilated conditions, and the largest environment cause of human mortality worldwide (WHO, 2009). Another example relates to over-harvesting forest resources which reduced the availability of the biomass resource for fuel and other purposes. Large scale biomass use also raises land use issues, particularly in instances where prime agricultural land is used for energy crops rather than food, and where forested land is converted to agricultural land for growing energy crops.

There is a great potential for sustainable improvements in renewable energy use and energy efficiency in developing countries as people rely primarily on solid fuels such as coal or wood for cooking. In addition to deploying smart grid technologies, energy policies in these countries should include a focus on developing off-grid renewable power and cooking/ heating technologies and on supporting energy efficiency programmes through capacity development and knowledge sharing (Stern, 2009 and IEA, 2010b).

Attention to local development dynamics is also vital. Increasing urban density and setting congestion charges can reduce energy and resource use without reducing economic growth. Findings from a general equilibrium model of OECD metropolitan regions demonstrate that urban density policies and congestion charges can reduce the overall cost to the economy of meeting greenhouse gas emissions reduction targets, compared to applying economy-wide policies, such as a carbon tax, alone (OECD, 2010n).[24] In this model, carbon emissions are reduced relative to the baseline following the implementation of densification policies[25] and congestion charges, a form of road toll of the type already implemented in London and Stockholm among others.[26] Strategic use of ecological infrastructure can also provide benefits in settled areas. Urban forests, grasslands, and wetlands enable water infiltration and transpiration, avoiding construction and maintenance costs of built infrastructure for storm water management. They provide climate regulating services, habitat for wildlife, and recreational opportunities, enhancing amenity values.

Transport

Green growth presents several challenges in relation to transport infrastructure. The first is ensuring continued levels of transport system performance to support economic growth and development. The embodied asset value of global paved-road and rail track capital stock in 2000 was estimated to be approximately USD 6 000 billion and was projected to grow by 41% by 2030 (OECD, 2006c).[27] Much of this growth is projected to take place outside the OECD area (Figure 2.10). Growth in OECD countries is projected to be relatively low and these economies are characterised by a large stock of mature existing infrastructure. Growth in demand in emerging economies is projected to be several orders of magnitude higher and decisions made during this high growth phase will shape patterns of use for decades to come (ITF, 2010a).

A second challenge relates to the deployment of infrastructure in support of new, potentially low-carbon transport technologies such as electric vehicles. Investment in high speed rail networks can also promote growth and yield environmental benefits, but only under the right conditions; evaluating when these conditions are met is critical.

Figure 2.10.   Projections for passenger and freight activity

All passenger travel, only heavy trucks and rail for freight travel

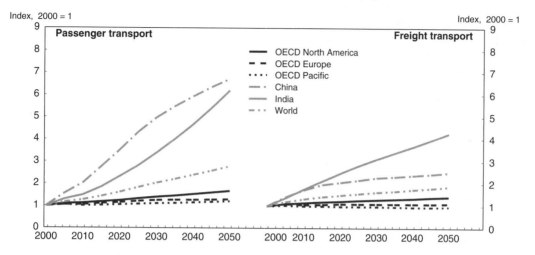

Source: Mobility Model (MoMo), IEA and ITF.

It is not clear what future energy and technology pathways will dominate the transport sector over the longer term and yet infrastructure investments today will continue to shape transport activity and demand well into the future. Transport infrastructure must allow networks to perform reliably over typical facility life-spans of 50 years or more in order to facilitate growth and other policy objectives. Green growth aspirations accentuate the need for governments to assess policies carefully, according to their long-term economic, environmental and social impacts.

Robust economic appraisal and cost benefit analysis is crucial. Appraisal techniques for public investments in transport are relatively mature but can be improved to take better account of uncertainty and make more explicit the contribution of potential investments to strategic policy goals (ITF, 2011a). Network infrastructure investment appraisal needs to be made on a life-cycle basis, covering maintenance as well as investment costs, and encompass network resilience and facility robustness to changing climate, as well as the costs of post-incident recovery.

If deep cuts are to be made to greenhouse gas emissions from transport, it is necessary to reduce the carbon-intensity of travel. The emerging view is that the focus should be first to improve the fuel efficiency of conventional engines and then gradually introduce alternative technologies (ITF, 2010b). At the same time, transport will need to make a shift away from a sole reliance on fossil energy to a broader range of fuel types and energy carriers. Electrification is likely to be a part of the shift (ITF, 2010c). Many authorities have commenced or are planning for a significant deployment of subsidies in support of consumer purchase of electric vehicles, charging infrastructure and smart-grid electricity distribution networks. Large-scale deployment of electric vehicles will require considerable public support until electric vehicle, battery and charging infrastructure cost and efficiency improvements are realised.[28] There is, however, a risk that public intervention in new energy distribution networks and technology may be costly either because it is premature or because it backs a technology that fails to win market support.

Electric cars generally represent a costly option for most consumers and society at present. However, under certain conditions, electric vehicles are nearly competitive with their internal combustion energy (ICE) counterparts. This is the case for urban delivery fleets and taxis where elevated daily travel distances (and avoided fossil fuel costs), relatively low cost electricity and the possibility for single-point fast charging systems already make up for the higher cost of electric vehicles. In these cases, the current generation of electric vehicles already makes sense from both an owner perspective (over a three-year payback period) and from a societal cost perspective. Subsidising a particular technology should always be subject to careful scrutiny and this is even more important where the technology already makes economic sense. Subsidies in support of charging infrastructure should also be weighed carefully. There is evidence that more deployment of expensive fast-charging infrastructure may be superfluous and in any case not necessary in the case of centrally managed electric vehicle fleets.[29]

It must also be kept in mind that lifecycle emissions from electric cars can be larger than comparable ICE models, depending on the carbon intensity of electricity generation. Furthermore, the comparison between ICE and electric vehicles may also turn less to the advantage of the electric vehicle over time in many regions since reducing the carbon intensity of electricity production may prove more difficult than improving the fuel efficiency of the combustion energy (GFEI, 2011).

High speed rail investments are another potential green growth project which figure prominently in many government investment programmes (*e.g.* France, Spain, United Kingdom, United States, China.) though some of the most ambitious plans have recently been scaled back (*e.g.* China). High speed rail can compete effectively with transport by passenger car and, more significantly, air over distances up to 1000 km where traffic is sufficiently dense, *i.e.* between major centres of population. For example, it holds over 90% of the combined air and rail markets between Paris and Lyon and Paris and Avignon. In general, where rail journey times can be brought close to three hours, high speed rail can be expected to take a major share of origin-destination aviation markets where demand is sufficiently high (approximately 9 million passengers per year) (Nash, 2009).

The benefits of high speed rail investments arise principally from time savings in relation to journeys by car or conventional rail, with benefits for both existing and new travellers, and relief of congestion on the conventional rail network and at airports. Wider economic benefits, through the effect of agglomeration, can arise but vary widely from case to case and unless the project radically transforms regional economic relations are generally a small part of overall benefits. In cases where anticipated journey volumes are low it is not only difficult to justify the investment in economic terms, but it may also be hard to defend the project from an environmental point of view as it will take too long for traffic to offset the emissions caused by building the line. Under such circumstances it may be better to upgrade a conventional line to increase capacity and accommodate somewhat higher speeds[30] (ITF, 2010a).

Environmental benefits are unlikely to be a significant part of the case for high-speed rail when all relevant factors are considered, but nor are they a strong argument against it provided that high load factors can be achieved and the infrastructure itself can be accommodated without excessive environmental damage to habitats, landscapes and neighbouring populations.

As much as green growth calls for changes in ways infrastructure is developed and used, in many respects the resolution of more conventional economic concerns are an equally important way forward. For instance, managing congestion is central to sustainable transport infrastructure policies. This issue is most prominent on the roads. Most studies of the external costs of road use find the cost of congestion to be many times larger than the cost of CO_2 emissions, even if the nature of the risks associated with climate change makes the comparison difficult. This is not to say that the cost of climate change is not large, rather there are also other pressing market failures in transport (Small and van Dender, 2007).

Green growth policies must address congestion not only because it hampers growth but also because congested road networks lead to increased GHG emissions. There is compelling evidence strengthening the case for using charges to bring congestion closer to efficient levels (ITF, 2010c). Dynamic user charging can help deliver more reliable and faster journey times and provides an effective mechanism for tempering increased travel demand that is often generated by new infrastructure.

Congestion charges, or distance-based charging, potentially raise substantial amounts of revenue. This is important since strong decarbonisation implies an erosion of fuel tax revenues which are a significant, stable and cheap source of public funds (van Dender and Crist, 2010). Charging systems, however, are also relatively costly to operate – much more so than current revenue raising mechanisms in transport – and this needs to be factored into transport planning and policy cost benefit analysis.

Water

Water resource management is a key component of green growth from several perspectives. It involves use of water for food production, industrial uses (*e.g.* cooling), drinking and sanitation, energy production, and recreational activities. It requires a consideration of watershed services in addition to water supply and sanitation. Currently 3 billion people have inadequate access to water. This is much more than an issue of availability. Without adequate investment in infrastructure, regulatory bodies, monitoring and information systems, lack of quality water services can be a significant constraint on growth. Properly managed, it can facilitate economic growth at minimal stress to natural systems.

However, ageing water infrastructure is increasingly a problem in developed countries. Some estimates suggest that the United States will have to invest USD 23 billion annually for the next 20 years to maintain water infrastructure at current service levels, while meeting health and environmental standards. Countries like the United Kingdom and Japan will need to increase their water spending by 20 to 40% to cope with urgent rehabilitation and upgrading of their water infrastructure.

In developing countries, USD 18 billion will be needed annually to extend existing infrastructure to achieve the water-related MDGs, roughly doubling current spending. An additional USD 54 billion per year will be needed just to ensure continued services to the currently served population (this does not include the additional needs generated by new infrastructure) (WHO, 2008).

The appropriate application of sustainable cost recovery for water and sanitation services can help meeting these infrastructure needs by providing revenues for government. The sources of finance for investment in water infrastructure and for operating and maintaining systems arise from tariffs, taxes, and transfers (official development assistance, ODA), otherwise known as the "3Ts". The balance between these three sources of finance varies significantly across OECD and non-OECD countries, and there is considerable scope for altering the mix of finance to meet fiscal and accessibility objectives. Figure 2.11 shows the shares of the 3Ts for selected countries in 2009.

Figure 2.11. **Financing of water supply and sanitation - sources of revenue**

Shares of tariffs, tax-based subsidies and ODA transfers[1]

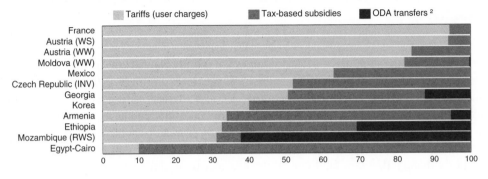

1. Data refer to different years, from 2005 to 2007.

2. Includes ODA grants as well as private grants, such as through non-governmental organisations. WS = Water Supply. WW = Waste Water. INV = Investment only. RWS = Rural Water Supply.

Source: OECD (2009), *Managing Water for All: An OECD Perspective on Pricing and Financing.*

StatLink http://dx.doi.org/10.1787/888932422230

Furthermore, investment in water infrastructure can reduce the strain on government health budgets by reducing external costs from adverse health impacts resulting from poor water and sanitation services. Almost 10% of the global burden of disease could be avoided through water and sanitation interventions and could result in several million lives being saved. In addition, there are benefits from time gains arising from not having to fetch water from long distances. Benefit-to-cost ratios have been reported to be as high as 7 to 1 for basic water and sanitation services in developing countries.

Wastewater treatment interventions that lead to improved water quality can also avoid significant costs. For instance, in Normandy (France), it has been estimated that non-compliance with bathing water norms resulting in closure of 40% of the coastal beaches would lead to a sudden drop of 14% of all visits. This would correspond to a loss of EUR 350 million per year and the potential loss of 2 000 local jobs. Losses on this scale are well worth avoiding.

Leveraging public and private sector finance

In most countries, the principal challenge for infrastructure is generating adequate financing. IEA estimates that providing universal access to electricity will require USD 33 billion per year up to 2030 (IEA, 2010b). In developing countries, the infrastructural deficit is particularly acute and investment demand to build, maintain or upgrade is immense. Between 1998 and 2007, spending on African infrastructure, for example, increased from USD 3 billion to USD 12 billion greatly exceeding average growth in infrastructure investment around the world. Many countries have announced even greater increases in such investments. For example, South Africa will invest USD 44 billion in transport, water and energy infrastructure between 2009 and 2011 – a 73 % increase in annual spending from 2007-2008 levels (Cloete *et al*, 2010).

In addition, it is estimated that adapting to and mitigating the effects of climate change over the next 40 years to 2050 will be in the order of USD 46 trillion or around USD 1 trillion a year (IEA, 2010b). While not all of this is infrastructure spending per se, much of it shares similar characteristics in terms of being for capital intensive and long-lived projects. Investment of this scale will require substantial private sources of financing.

With their USD 28 trillion in assets, pension funds - along with other institutional investors - can have an important role to play in this regard. Green infrastructure projects (such as non-carbon energy production, carbon sequestration, reforestation, water treatment, waste recycling etc.) are - in theory at least- interesting to pension funds as long-term investors looking for instruments which provide inflation protection, a steady yield and which have a low correlation to the rest of their portfolio. However, in practice, pension funds' asset allocation to infrastructure in general is less than 1% in most countries. Governments have a role to play in ensuring that attractive opportunities and instruments are available to pension funds and institutional investors in order to be able to tap into this source of capital (IOPS, 2011; Inderst, 2010).

Clear and consistent policies over a long period of time are needed so that strategic and financial players have the confidence to invest in green growth projects. Before private investors will commit large amounts of capital to this sector there must be transparent, long-term and certain regulations governing carbon emissions, renewable energy and energy efficiency. Governments and regulators should also revisit regulation to make sure it is not inadvertently discouraging pension funds from investing in long-term projects, which green projects will often require. As an example, recent changes in both pension regulatory frameworks and accounting rules in the OECD area (the Pension Protection Act of 2006, FAB 158 in US and IAS19) have put increasing pressure to reduce funding gaps in defined benefit plans (OECD, 2011g). Such changes (including the move to market to market accounting) ironically may be forcing pension funds into shorter-term assets and into matching their liabilities with government bonds (which require the smallest solvency buffers).[31]

To leverage financing from more diffuse or smaller sources requires structured instruments such as green bonds and green funds. The market size for all green bond issuances to date is approximately USD 11 billion (with USD 1.9 billion issued by the World Bank alone), a drop in the ocean (0.012%) of the capital held in the global bond markets, estimated to be worth USD 91 trillion globally (OECD, 2011g). There is scope for scaled up issuances of green bonds (in the hundreds of billions per year) but if this capital is to be raised through a thriving and liquid green bond market, transparent policies based on long term, comprehensive and ambitious political commitment are needed. The recent United Kingdom political commitment to a Green Investment Bank is a strong step in this direction; the Bank is expected to be able to start issuing bonds by 2015 (HM Treasury, 2011).

Infrastructure financing is often seen to be risky, largely as a result of regulatory risk. Governments therefore also need to find ways to make infrastructure investment attractive by mitigating these risks without removing incentives to manage risk. One tool for this is to use public-private partnerships (PPP) in infrastructure provision where the presence of a commercial partner can help to reduce the regulatory risk.

PPPs are, however, no panacea. They need to be carefully managed and a number of conditions have to be in place to make co-operation between the public and the private sector work. They include a sound institutional and regulatory environment for infrastructure investment; administrative capacities to develop and oversee projects; transparency; and appropriate contractual arrangements In particular, contracts need to specify outputs rather than inputs. Therefore, in projects where it is hard to specify the output – such as in areas of rapid technological progress – PPPs are likely to be less appropriate (OECD, 2007).

Other innovations can be used to mobilise market-based finance to fund infrastructure development, depending on the kinds of financing barriers that exist. One example is the combining of concessionary financing (either grants or loans with a grant element) with repayable finance in order to support a single project or a comprehensive lending program.

For countries with underdeveloped capital markets, ODA will be an important source of investment capital. However, ODA is limited by pressures on government budgets in donor countries and it is dwarfed by private capital flows in the aggregate global context (Gentry, 1999). In the last decade, FDI has increased dramatically relative to ODA. More specifically in industries that contribute most to climate change and in other polluting sectors FDI flows greatly exceed ODA and export credits specifically targeted at these industries (Corfee-Morlot, Guay and Larsen, 2009).

Beyond this global picture, in many poor developing countries ODA exceeds FDI and thus remains an important source of finance for green investments. ODA targeted to environmental purposes amounted to USD 26 billion in 2009, a 45 % increase from 2007. In addition, there is more than USD 10 billion under operation in various climate funds, and developed countries committed to make USD 30 billion available as "fast-start" finance in 2010- 2012 and USD 100 billion per year by 2020. [32]

However, there is still the need to build confidence in the delivery of these green funds over the long-term and to ensure effective use. Experience suggests that the effective use of external funding would require that the sources of finance are not fragmented and that financing goes through national budgetary process of recipient countries in line with their own development plans.

Official export credits could also generate new sources of funding and stimulate private investment in developing countries. In recent years, the majority of the medium and long term official export credits flows that go from OECD governments to developing countries have supported the transport (36%) and industry (26%) sectors, followed by energy projects (11%). However, the proportion of flows going to low-carbon projects remains a minor share of official export credits; for example, renewable energies represent only USD 0.7 billion and less than 2% of the total. Latest steps taken by countries to encourage environmental accountability in official export credits could contribute to the financing of green investment plans. These include the liberalisation of special rules governing the provision of support for renewable energy and water projects as well as recent negotiations to consider whether and how key sectors and technologies could become eligible for favourable financial terms and conditions.

Institutions and governance

Institutional and governance capacity to implement wide-ranging policy reform is an essential condition for greening growth. Governments need to be able to integrate green growth objectives into broader economic policymaking and development planning (Box 2.5). Developing such capacity is a key structural issue and applies as much to many OECD countries as it does to developing countries. This issue is not restricted to formal national level planning processes, such as national plans or poverty reduction strategies (PRSPs), but extends to public financial management (especially the budget process), developing strategies for key economic sectors as well as how these feed through into sub-national development. It concerns not only policy priorities but also the choice and design of programmes, public investments and regulation of economic activity.

For some countries, building capacity to improve the governance and oversight of natural assets and to enforce policies will be the central feature of green growth. Often pressure on natural resources appears to come from external pressures, such as export demand, but this is a result of relatively weak governance and the prevalence of open-access to natural resources (Fischer, 2010).

This is not necessarily a case for strengthening governance from the top-down. Policies that respect both formal and informal resource user rights can strengthen resource governance institutions. In this context, an essential element of managing shared natural resource is co-operation and collective action by stakeholders.

Capacity development for green growth policies should take a "country system approach" across government. It will be all but impossible to achieve if finance and core economic ministries are not playing a leading role. While the policy motivation for greener growth may lie in environmental concerns, green growth policies are not exclusively environmental policies. They should be core economic policies that have engaged   central planning, finance and sectoral ministries as well as environment agencies in their formulation. The role and capacity of non-governmental actors in the private sector and civil society will also be important.

Box 2.5. Green growth objectives and national development planning

The **National Strategy for Green Growth and the Five-Year Plan (2009-2013) of Korea** provide a comprehensive policy framework for green growth. The Strategy aims to: (1) promote eco-friendly new growth engines, (2) enhance peoples' quality of life, and (3) contribute to the international efforts to fight climate change. To facilitate the realisation of the new vision, the Presidential Commission on Green Growth was established in 2009 and The Framework Act on Low Carbon Green Growth was enacted in January 2010. Drawing on the planning practice that was discontinued in the early 1990s, the Five-Year Plan (2009-2013) provides a blueprint for government actions for implementation of the Strategy; containing specific budget earmarks and detailed tasks for line ministries and local governing entities. Under the plan, the government will spend about 2% of the annual GDP on green growth programs and projects (*e.g.* on green infrastructures and R&D of green technologies).

The **National Development Plan of Ireland** (2007-2013) sets out indicative financial allocations for the investment priorities aimed at enhancing economic competitiveness and at providing a better quality of life. It brings together different sectoral investment policies into one overall framework, in order to promote co-ordination and alignment between sectoral policies, providing a financial framework within which government departments and agencies can plan and deliver the implementation of public investment. The Plan emphasises the importance attached to several horizontal themes, including environmental sustainability. The environment chapter covers transport, waste management, climate change, environmental research, and sustainable energy. The NDP set out a strong financial framework to enable Ireland to tackle environmental challenges over the period 2007-13. In 2007, investment programmes with a direct impact on promoting environmental sustainability exceeded EUR 1.3 billion.

The "Green Development" section of **China's 12th Five Year Plan** (FYP, 2011-2015) is a manifestation of the country's aspiration to move towards a greener economy. The Plan is a strategic national roadmap, setting priorities regarding China's future socioeconomic development, and providing guidelines and targets for policy making at sectoral and sub-national level. The "Green Development" theme has identified six strategic pillars: climate change, resource saving and management, circular economy, environmental protection, ecosystem protection and recovery, water conservation and natural disaster prevention. These pillars entail several new binding targets, *e.g.* carbon emission per unit GDP to be reduced by 17% by 2015, NO_x and ammonia nitrogen emissions to be reduced by 10% by 2015, in addition to targets continued from 11th FYP, *e.g.* energy intensity, SO_2 and COD pollution. Detailed policy guidelines have also been provided in the 12th FYP, for instance, energy-efficiency technology demonstration and diffusion programs have been emphasised as the engine of both energy saving and new growth opportunities.

The **Economic Development and Poverty Reduction Strategy of Rwanda** (2008-2012) represents the country's second medium-term strategy towards the attainment of the long-term Rwanda Vision 2020 Objectives. The EDPRS sets out medium-term objectives and indicative financial allocations. Environment is identified as a key cross-cutting issue. In addition several sectors with a strong environmental and natural resource content have been identified as critical for achieving Rwanda's development objectives, given their links to productive (*e.g.* land) or to health (*e.g.* water supply and sanitation). The Environment, Land and Forestry sector has been allocated for the period 2008-2012 a total of RWF 62 billion (Rwandan francs), representing 1.8% of total public expenditure, while its share of total capital expenditure amount to 3.8%. In turn, the Water and Sanitation sector has been allocated a total of RWF 146 billion, representing 4.2% of total expenditure, with the share of capital expenditure amounting to 5.5%.

Source: People's Republic of China (2011), "The Twelfth Five-Year Plan for National Economic and Social Development of The People's Republic of China", Government of Ireland (2008), "Ireland National Development Plan 2007-2013. Transforming Ireland A Better Quality of Life for All". Annual Report 2007, and Government of Rwanda (2008), Economic Development and Poverty Reduction Strategy.

Neither can green growth rely solely on institutions at the level of central government. Effective governance across different levels of government will be key. Urban initiatives both affect and are affected by economy-wide fiscal policies and national sectoral policies (particularly transportation, building, labour, innovation and education policy). There are cases in which national-level policies can undermine regional level green growth policies due to the lack of information on conflicting rules or practices. Similarly, regional initiatives that focus on stand-alone or "flagship" projects without regard to where these projects fit within national policy frameworks risk falling short of their promise.

Moreover, multi-level governance is of considerable practical importance for guiding investment and innovation in a number of key areas such as water and sanitation systems. Affecting changes in a cost-effective manner requires ongoing co-ordination across ministries, public agencies and between levels of government involved in policymaking.

Overlapping jurisdictional authorities can undermine the cost-effectiveness of policies if not managed. If, for example, the stringency of a federal cap and trade scheme varied by state, the end result, compared with a federal-only policy, would most likely be more emissions in lax states, the same total national emissions, and less cost efficiency. This can be overcome, in certain circumstances, by essentially "carving out" a more stringent state-level policy from the national policy, resulting in two distinct policies that no longer overlap.

State-level policies can, however, be beneficial in the presence of federal policy. First, states can correct market failures not addressed by federal policy. For example, renters whose utilities are not separately metered have little incentive to conserve electricity; this "agency" problem can be addressed through local building codes. Second, states can serve as testing grounds for novel policies and inform future federal policy development. Third, stringent state-level policy can lead by putting pressure on federal policy makers. Finally, stringent state-level policies can pressure manufacturers to adopt the tighter standards nationwide.

Green growth strategies need to provide a degree of policy stability beyond electoral cycles. One way to achieve this is to entrench policy strategies into the statutory or regulatory environment and establish independent institutions. One example of this is the legislation of climate targets in the United Kingdom and the independent Climate Committee established under the Climate Change Act to advise government on policy and progress towards these targets. Institutions which are independent of executive government and which have a clear regulatory mandate, much as central banks often do, are also important for providing a degree of flexibility in policymaking. This can allow policy to be shifted as new technologies or policy innovation emerges. It can also allow countries to adapt to positive and negative shocks in global and domestic environmental and economic conditions without compromising long-term goals or creating excess uncertainty about the future of policy.

More generally, the independence of regulators is central to preventing the regulator from being "captured" by industry or partisan political interests and enhances the stability and credibility of the regulatory framework, in a context where accountability to the government, the legislature and consumers should nonetheless be preserved. Independence facilitates information sharing between regulated firms and regulators and empirical analysis also demonstrates that independence of the regulator is associated with higher investment, presumably reflecting the effect of greater predictability and credibility (OECD, 2009c).

Notes

[1] These elements of policy design and the following discussion on strengths and weaknesses of different policy instruments is drawn from de Serres, Murtin and Nicoletti (2010).

[2] The statistical data for Israel are supplied by and under the responsibility of the relevant Israeli authorities. The use of such data by the OECD is without prejudice to the status of the Golan Heights, East Jerusalem and Israeli settlements in the West Bank under the terms of international law.

[3] See, for example, OECD (2005) and OECD (2011a).

[4] The OECD is developing measurement methods to help enhance transparency around support for fossil fuels, and is starting to collect data on subsidies and tax expenditures that encourage fossil fuel use or production in OECD countries. Where data do exist, they reveal that the tax expenditures range from minor relief to selected consumers or industries to broad relief to all taxpayers. The special rules and tax advantages that give rise to these indirect subsidies can be relatively subtle and complex, making them less apparent than direct subsidies to fossil-fuel prices.

[5] This issue is on the current agenda of the G20 countries, who on 25 September 2009 stated they "commit to rationalise and phase out over the medium term inefficient fossil fuel subsidies that encourage wasteful consumption" (G20, 2009). A key challenge in this effort will be finding effective alternative mechanisms (*e.g.* means-tested social safety net programmes) for assisting low-income consumers that benefit from existing subsidies, particularly in developing countries where traditional tax and transfer institutions are less reliable.

[6] Such as market price support and associated trade barriers, direct production support, or input subsidies.

[7] Inflexible regulatory standards may of course be the only option applicable when a complete ban on certain activities is necessary.

[8] Other issues include small farm holdings and thus high transactions costs. These reasons and a frequent lack of access to credit also help explain why there is limited participation by the poor in PES programmes. While the development of PES is desirable, the impact on poverty is reduced because of a variety of obstacles.

[9] For wide-ranging analysis of the effectiveness of voluntary agreements in OECD countries, refer to OECD (2003).

[10] Conversely, a lack of competitive pressure is often found to be reflected in weaker investment (Alesina *et al.*, 2005), weaker efficiency gains (Nickell, Nicolitsas and Dryden, 1997; Nicoletti and Scarpetta, 2003) and, at least over a range, weaker innovation (Aghion and Howitt, 2005; Griffith, Harrison and Simpson, 2006). In this regard it is an important condition for green growth in both OECD and major emerging economies (see also Conway, Dougherty and Radziwill, 2010).

[11] Wind-based energy can be much better predicted 3 hours before it is produced than a day before it is produced. Therefore, if bidding rules for system operators involve day-ahead bidding (as opposed to short-advance bidding) wind will be disadvantaged. In contrast, other generators who need to plan human resources in advance may face difficulties from short-notice bidding that is ongoing during a day. For more on these and related issues in energy networks see *e.g.* OECD (2010f).

12   The first possibility is to require new entrants to buy the additional permits entirely within the market (as in the United States SO_2 emission trading scheme). The second possibility is to hold a reserve of permits that are allocated to new entrants for free (as in the EU-ETS). Conversely, the question is how to deal with the emission permits of firms that close down or significantly reduce their capacity. In this case, firms may still receive and sell their permits for a certain period. Under the United States SO_2 emission trading scheme, for example, this period is 30 years. Alternatively, they may be obliged to give away their permits to the government, as is the case in most European countries (see OECD, 2011b).

13   For a discussion on the drivers of growth including the implications of openness to trade and FDI in OECD and major emerging economies see Bouis, Duval and Murtin (2011).

14   The extent of environmental impacts and gains from trade can be further reviewed in work by the OECD Joint Working Party on Trade and the Environment, for example.

15   See discussion in OECD (2011c).

16   Importantly, Weitzman (2009) concludes: "…the economic consequences of fat-tailed structural uncertainty (along with unsureness about high-temperature damages) can readily outweigh the effects of discounting in climate-change policy analysis."

17   In France, the General Directorate for Fair Trading, Consumer Affairs and Fraud Control has launched a website comparing the rates and other characteristics of all the electricity and gas contracts offered on the French market (OECD, 2010h). In Slovenia, the National Energy Regulator introduced an online tool which enables consumers to calculate and monitor their monthly electricity consumption and check the accuracy of their monthly bills (OECD, 2010h).

18   Such a "backstop technology" refers to a technology or process that is capable of meeting the demand requirements and has a virtually infinite resource base. The concept was introduced by Nordhaus (1973).

19   Note by Turkey: The information in this document with reference to "Cyprus" relates to the southern part of the Island. There is no single authority representing both Turkish and Greek Cypriot people on the Island. Turkey recognizes the Turkish Republic of Northern Cyprus (TRNC). Until a lasting and equitable solution is found within the context of the United Nations, Turkey shall preserve its position concerning the "Cyprus" issue.

20   Note by all the European Union Member States of the OECD and the European Commission: The Republic of Cyprus is recognized by all members of the United Nations with the exception of Turkey. The information in this document relates to the area under the effective control of the Government of the Republic of Cyprus.

21   The statistical data for Israel are supplied by and under the responsibility of the relevant Israeli authorities. The use of such data by the OECD is without prejudice to the status of the Golan Heights, East Jerusalem and Israeli settlements in the West Bank under the terms of international law.

22   Generally, feed-in tariffs refer to the regulatory, minimum guaranteed price that is paid to a private, independent producer that generates electricity using renewable energy. Occasionally, FITs mean the full price per kWh received by the producers, including the premium above or additional to the market price, but excluding tax rebates or other subsidies paid by the government (Sijm, 2002).

23   One estimate is that the energy contained in all fossil fuel burned in 1997 was equivalent to 400 hundred years of primary productivity from photosynthesis (Dukes, 2003).

24   More precisely, this modelling exercise has been carried out by employing the spatialised version of the IMACLIM-R CGE framework (Crassous, Hourcade and Sassi, 2006). IMACLIM-R allows simulating the interactions between changes in energy consumption, carbon emissions and economic growth, given a set of policies and other exogenous factors. Special thanks are given to Fabio Grazi

and Henri Waisman (CIRED) for modelling work with IMACLIM-R and the urban module that incorporates the OECD metropolitan database.

[25] Densification indicates policies that increase the number of people per square kilometre in a given urban area. These include restrictive policies, which actively pursue densification such as through green belt policies, and enabling policies, which allow activity to be drawn to the core such as public transportation systems or the elimination of distortions in the market such as taxes for deconcentration.

[26] Such a road toll reduces average rather than marginal commuting costs by car (see Henderson (1974) for the underlying economics of road pricing mechanisms).

[27] These figures do not include other significant (*e.g.* tunnels, bridges and pipelines) or regionally important (gravel and ice roads) surface transport infrastructure. Nor do these figures account for the significant sunken investment in ports, causeways, levees, locks and airports.

[28] Many governments are currently funding the creation of markets for electric vehicles. The subsidies available per vehicle can be large, and depending on the vehicle purchased are currently over USD 7 000 in Belgium, Canada (Quebec and Ontario), China, the Netherlands, the United Kingdom and the United States. The United Kingdom, for example, has made provisions for more than GBP 400 million (EUR 472 million) to support research, infrastructure installation, and provide consumer incentives. As part of its Integral Strategy to promote the electric vehicle, Spain will be investing EUR 215 million in 2011 to support forward-looking investments by vehicle and parts' manufacturers. This public financing is expected to mobilise EUR 1 738 million private investment.

[29] Evidence from consumer trials indicate that expensive fast-charging infrastructure has been much demanded before the trials but little used during the trials since consumers found that typical slow (and less expensive) charging infrastructure was sufficient for their travel needs (Turrentine (2010) – personal communication based on BMW Mini E field trial analysis).

[30] Energy consumption increases with the square of the speed.

[31] See for further reference; Yermo, J. and C. Severinson (2010) and Impavido and Tower (2009).

[32] For regularly updated information on climate funds see www.climatefundsupdate.org.

References

Aghion, P and P. Howitt (2005), "Appropriate Growth Policy: A Unifying Framework", *The Joseph Schumpeter Lecture,* paper presented at the 20th Annual Congress of the European Economic Association, Amsterdam, August 25, 2005.

Alesina, A., S. Ardagna, G. Nicoletti and F. Schiantarelli (2005), "Regulation and Investment", *Journal of the European Economic Association*, Vol. 3, No. 4, Wiley Blackwell, Zurich, pp. 791-825.

Anthoff, D. and R. Hahn (2010), "Government Failure and Market Failure: On the Inefficiency of Environmental and Energy Policy", *Oxford Review of Economic Policy*, Vol. 26, No. 2, Oxford University Press, Oxford, pp.197–224.

Arnason, R, K. Kelleher and R. Willmann (2008). *The Sunken Billions: The Economic Justification for Fisheries Reform,* World Bank and FAO, Washington DC, available at http://go.worldbank.org/MGUTHSY7U0.

Beaton, C and L. Lontoh (2010), "Lessons Learned from Indonesia's Attempts to Reform Fossil-Fuel Subsidies", International Institute for Sustainable Development, Winnipeg.

Bouis, R., R. Duval and F. Murtin (2011), "The Policy and Institutional Drivers of Economic Growth Across OECD and Non-OECD Economies: New Evidence from Growth Regressions", *OECD Economics Department Working Papers*, No. 843, OECD, Paris.

Bumbudsanpharoke, W. (2010), "Behaviours and Attitudes in the Management of Nonpoint Source Pollution: Ping River Basin, Thailand", PhD Thesis, University of Edinburgh, Edinburgh.

CGP (Commissariat Général du Plan) (2005), "Révision du taux d'actualisation des investissements publics : rapport du groupe d'experts présidé par Daniel Lebègue" (Revision of the Discount Rate of Public Investment : Report of the Group of Experts headed by Daniel Lebègue), 21 janvier 2005, Commissariat Général du Plan, Paris.

Cloete, R., F. Faulhaber and M. Zils (2010), "Infrastructure: A Long Road Ahead", *The McKinsey Quarterly*, available at www.mckinseyquarterly.com.

Conway, P., S. Dougherty and A. Radziwill (2010), "Longterm Growth and Policy Challenges in the Large Emerging Economies", *OECD Economics Department Working Papers*, No. 755, OECD, Paris.

Corfee-Morlot, J., B. Guay and K. M. Larsen (2009), "Financing Climate Change Mitigation: Towards a Framework for Measurement, Reporting, and Verification", OECD-IEA, Paris, available at www.oecd.org/dataoecd/0/60/44019962.pdf.

Cotis, J-P., A. de Serres and R. Duval (2010), "Competitiveness, Economic Performance and Structural Policies: An OECD Perspective", in P. De Grauwe (ed.), *The Many Dimensions of Competitiveness*, MIT Press, Cambridge.

Crassous, R., J.C. Hourcade and O. Sassi (2006), "Endogenous Structural Change and Climate Targets: Modeling Experiments within IMACLIM-R", *The Energy Journal*, Special Issue No.1, International Association for Energy Economics, Ohio, pp. 259-276.

De Mello, L. (2010), "Enhancing the Effectiveness of Social Policies in Indonesia", *OECD Economics Department Working Papers*, No. 810, OECD, Paris.

De Serres, A, F. Murtin and G. Nicoletti (2010), "A Framework for Assessing Green Growth Policies", *OECD Economics Department Working Papers*, No. 774, OECD, Paris.

Dechezlepretre A., M. Glachant, I. Hascic, N. Johnstone and Y. Ménière (2011), "Invention and Transfer of Climate Change Mitigation Technologies: A Global Analysis" in *Review of Environmental Economics and Policy* (forthcoming).

Dukes, J.S. (2003), "Burning Buried Sunshine: Human Consumption of Ancient Solar Energy", *Climatic Change*, Vol. 61, No. 1-2, Springer Science + Business Media, Inc., Heidelberg, pp. 31-44.

ECF (European Climate Foundation) (2010), "Roadmap 2050", European Climate Foundation, The Hague, available at www.roadmap2050.eu.

EU (2009), "Directive 2009/72/EC of the European Parliament and of the Council of 13 July 2009 Concerning Common Rules for the Internal Market in Electricity and repealing Directive 2003/54/EC" , European Union, Brussels.

EU (European Union) (2006), "Directive 2006/32/EC of the European Parliament and of the Council of 5 April 2006, on Energy End-Use Efficiency and Energy Services and repealing Council Directive 93/76/EEC" , European Union, Brussels.

Fischer, C. and L. Preonas (2010), "Combining Policies for Renewable Energy: Is the Whole Less than the Sum of Its Parts?" *Discussion Paper* 10-19, Resources for the Future, Washington DC.

Fischer, C. (2010), "Does Trade Help or Hinder the Conservation of Natural Resources?" *Review of Environmental Economics and Policy*, Vol. 4, Issue 1, Winter 2010, Wiley Online Library, New Jersey, pp. 103–121.

G20 (2009), *Leaders' Statement: The Pittsburgh Summit,* 25 September 2009, Pittsburgh Summit, Pittsburgh available at www.pittsburghsummit.gov/mediacenter/129639.htm.

Gentry, B. S. (1999), Private Capital Flows and the Environment: Lessons from Latin America, Edward Elgar Publishing, Cheltenham.

GFEI (2011), "50by50 Prospects and Progress", prepared by George Eads, Global Fuel Economy Initiative, London, available at www.globalfueleconomy.org/Documents/Publications/prospects_and_progress_lr.pdf.

Goerres, A. (2006), "The Tragic Paradox: Germany's Very Successful but Not Very Popular Green Budget Reform", *Green Budget Paper,* No. 2006/12, Green Budget Germany, Berlin.

Government of Ireland (2008), "Ireland National Development Plan 2007-2013. Transforming Ireland A Better Quality of Life for All", *Annual Report 2007*, Government of Ireland, Dublin.

Government of Rwanda (2008), *Economic Development and Poverty Reduction Strategy*, Government of Rwanda, Kigali.

Griffith, R., R. Harrison and H. Simpson (2006), "Product Market Reform and Innovation in the EU", *CEPR Discussion Papers,* No. 5849, Centre for Economic Policy Research, Washington DC.

Haščič, I. and N. Johnstone (2011), "The Clean Development Mechanism and International Technology Transfer: Empirical Evidence on Wind Power", *Climate Policy* (forthcoming).

Henderson, V. (1974), "Road Congestion. A Reconsideration of Pricing Theory", *Journal of Urban Economics*, Vol. 1, No. 3, Elsevier, Amsterdam, pp. 346–365.

Hepburn, C. (2007), "Use of Discount Rates in the Estimation of the Costs of Inaction with Respect to Selected Environmental Concerns", *OECD Environment Paper*, Vol. 7, No. 9, OECD, Paris.

HM Treasury (2011), "Budget 2011", HM Treasury, London, available at www.hm-treasury.gov.uk/2011budget.htm.

Houde, S. and A. Todd (2010), "List of Behavioral Economic Principles that can Inform Energy Policy", Precourt Energy Efficiency Center at Stanford University, (work in progress) available at www.stanford.edu/~annitodd/List_of_Behavioral_Economic_Principles_for_Energy_Programs.pdf.

ICPEN (International Consumer Protection and Enforcement Network) (2010), www.icpen.org

IEA (2010a), *World Energy Outlook*, OECD/IEA, Paris.

IEA (2010b), *Energy Technology Perspectives*, OECD/IEA, Paris.

IEA (2011), RD&D Budget Database, IEA, Paris.

IEA, OPEC, OECD, World Bank (2010), "Analysis of the Scope of Energy Subsidies and Suggestions for the G20 Initiative", prepared for the G20 Summit, Seoul, 11-12 November 2010, available at www.oecd.org/g20/fossilfuelsubsidies.

Igami, M. and A. Saka (2007), "Capturing the Evolving Nature of Science, the Development of New Scientific Indicators and The Mapping of Science", *OECD Science, Technology and Industry Working Papers*, No. 2007/1, OECD, Paris.

Impavido, G. and I. Tower (2009), "How the Financial Crisis Affects Pensions and Insurance and Why the Impacts Matter", *IMF Working Paper,* IMF, Washington DC, available at www.imf.org/external/pubs/ft/wp/2009/wp09151.pdf

Inderst, G. (2010), "Infrastructure as an Asset Class", *EIB Papers,* Volume 15 No.1, European Investment Bank, Luxembourg, pp. 70-105, available at http://www.eib.org/attachments/efs/eibpapers/eibpapers_2010_v15_n01_en.pdf#page=72

IOPS (2011), "Pension Fund Use of Alternative Investments and Derivatives: Regulation, Industry Practice and Implementation Issues", The International Organisation of Pension Supervisors (forthcoming).

ITF (International Transport Forum) (2010a), *Transport Outlook 2010: The Potential for Innovation*, OECD, Paris, summary available at www.internationaltransportforum.org/Pub/pdf/10Outlook.pdf

ITF (2010b), "Stimulating Low-Carbon Vehicle Technologies", *Discussion Paper*, No. 2010-13, ITF, OECD, Paris, summary available at www.internationaltransportforum.org/jtrc/DiscussionPapers/DP201013.pdf.

ITF (2010c), "Implementing Congestion Charges", *Discussion Paper*, No. 2010-12 ITF, OECD, Paris, summary available at www.internationaltransportforum.org/jtrc/DiscussionPapers/DP201012.pdf.

ITF (2011a), "Improving the Practice of Transport Appraisal", *Discussion Paper*, No. 2011-01 ITF, OECD, Paris, summary available at www.internationaltransportforum.org/jtrc/DiscussionPapers/DP201101.pdf.

Johnstone, N. (2007), *Corporate Behaviour and Environmental Policy*, Edward Elgar, Cheltenham and OECD, Paris.

Johnstone, N. and I. Haščič (2011), "The Benefits of Fostering Innovation in Storage and Grid Management Technologies under Imperfect Information", *OECD Environment Working Papers* (forthcoming).

Johnstone, N., I. Haščič and D. Popp (2010), "Renewable Energy Policies and Technological Innovation: Evidence Based on Patent Counts", in *Environmental and Resource Economics*, Vol. 45, Issue 1, pp. 133-155.

Lawson, A. and N.M. Bird (2008), "Government Institutions, Public Expenditure and the Role of Development Partners: Meeting the New Environmental Challenges of the Developing World", Final report to DFOD/CIDA/UNEP, Overseas Development Institute, London, available at www.odi.org.uk/fecc/resources/reports/s0166_final_report.pdf.

Lewis, J. I. and R. H. Wiser (2007), "Fostering a Renewable Energy Technology Industry: An International Comparison of Wind Industry Policy Support Mechanisms", *Energy Policy*, Vol. 35, Elsevier, Amsterdam, pp. 1844-1857.

Lipp, J. (2007), "Lessons for Effective Renewable Electricity Policy from Denmark, Germany and the United Kingdom", *Energy Policy,* Vol. 35, No. 11, Elsevier, Amsterdam, pp. 5481–5495.

Maskus, K. (2010), "Differentiated Intellectual Property Regimes for Environmental and Climate Technologies", *OECD Environment Working Papers,* No. 17, OECD, Paris.

Mourougane, A. (2010), "Phasing Out Energy Subsidies in Indonesia", *OECD Economics Department Working Papers*, No. 808, OECD, Paris.

Nash, C. (2009), "When to Invest in High-Speed Rail Links and Networks?" in *The Future for Interurban Passenger Transport*, International Transport Forum/OECD, Paris, available at http://internationaltransportforum.org/jtrc/DiscussionPapers/DP200916.pdf.

Newell, R. G. and N. E. Wilson (2005), "Technology Prizes for Climate Change Mitigation", *Discussion Paper* 05-33, Resources for the Future, Washington DC.

Nickell, S., D. Nicolitsas and N. Dryden (1997), "What Makes Firms Perform Well?", *European Economic Review*, Vol. 41, Elsevier, Amsterdam, pp 783–796.

Nicoletti, G. and S. Scarpetta (2003), "Regulation, Productivity and Growth", *Economic Policy*, Vol. 36, Wiley-Blackwell, New Jersey, pp. 11-72.

Nordhaus, W. (1973), "The Allocation of Energy Reserves", *Brookings Papers* No. 3, Brookings Institution, Washington DC, pp. 529-570.

OECD (2003), *Voluntary Approaches for Environmental Policy: Effectiveness, Efficiency, and Usage in Policy Mixes*, OECD, Paris.

OECD (2004), *The Economic Impact of ICT: Measurement, Evidence and Implications*, OECD, Paris.

OECD (2005), "Environmental Fiscal Reform for Poverty Reduction", *DAC Guidelines and Reference Series*, OECD, Paris.

OECD (2006a), *OECD Employment Outlook: Boosting Jobs and Incomes*, OECD, Paris.

OECD (2006b), *Cost-Benefit Analysis and the Environment: Recent Developments*, OECD, Paris.

OECD (2006c), *Infrastructure to 2030: Telecom, Land Transport, Water and Electricity*, OECD, Paris.

OECD (2007a), *Principles for Private Sector Participation in Infrastructure*, available at www.oecd.org/daf/investment/ppp.

OECD (2008), *Costs of Inaction on Key Environmental Challenges*, OECD, Paris.

OECD (2009a), *Indicators of Regulatory Management Systems*, OECD, Paris.

OECD (2009b), *Promoting Consumer Education, Trends, Policies and Good Practices*, OECD, Paris.

OECD (2009c), *Economic Policy Reforms 2009: Going for Growth*, OECD, Paris.

OECD (2009d), *Managing Water for All: An OECD Perspective on Pricing and Financing*, OECD, Paris.

OECD (2010a), *Taxation, Innovation and the Environment*, OECD, Paris.

OECD (2010b), *Green Growth Strategy Interim Report: Implementing our Commitment for a Sustainable Future*, Document prepared for the Meeting of the OECD Council at Ministerial Level, 27-28 May 2010, OECD, Paris.

OECD (2010c), "Tax Policy Reform and Economic Growth", *OECD Tax Policy Studies,* No. 20, OECD, Paris.

OECD (2010d), *Sustainable Management of Water Resources in Agriculture*, OECD, Paris.

OECD (2010e), *Economic Outlook,* No. 88, OECD, Paris.

OECD (2010f), "Smart Grids and Renewable Energy", OECD Competition Committee Roundtable, OECD, Paris.

OECD (2010g), "Enhancing the Value and Effectiveness of Environmental Claims: Protecting and Empowering Consumers", Report on OECD Workshop, OECD, Paris.

OECD (2010h), *Consumer Policy Toolkit*, OECD, Paris.

OECD (2010i), "Environmental Claims: Findings and Conclusions of the Committee of the OECD Committee on Consumer Policy", OECD, Paris.

OECD (2010j), *The OECD Innovation Strategy: Getting a Head Start on Tomorrow*, OECD, Paris.

OECD (2010k), *Measuring Innovation – A New Perspective*, OECD, Paris.

OECD (2010l), *Sustainable Chemistry: Evidence on Innovation from Patent Data*, Draft report to the Joint Meeting of the Chemicals Committee and the Working Party on Chemicals, Pesticides and Biotechnology, OECD, Paris.

OECD (2010n), *Eco-Innovation in Industry: Enabling Green Growth*, OECD, Paris.

OECD (2010o), *Cities and Climate Change*, OECD, Paris.

OECD (2011a), "Draft Policy Guidance on Capacity Development for Environment" (forthcoming).

OECD (2011b), "Emission Permit Trading and Competition", OECD Competition Committee Roundtable (forthcoming).

OECD (2011c), "Defining and Measuring Green FDI: Preliminary Findings and Issues for Discussion" (forthcoming).

OECD (2011d), *Greening Household Behaviour: The Role of Public Policy*, OECD, Paris.

OECD (2011e), "Fostering Innovation for Green Growth" (forthcoming).

OECD (2011f). "Directing Technological Change while Reducing the Risk of (not) Picking Winners: The Case of Renewable Energy" (forthcoming).

OECD (2011g), "Pension Fund Investment in Infrastructure: Policy Recommendations" (forthcoming).

OECD (2011h), *Patent Database*. OECD, Paris, available at www.oecd.org/document/41/0,3746,en_2649_34451_40813225_1_1_1_1,00.html.

OECD (2011i), *Research and Development Statistics Database*, OECD, Paris.

OECD (2011j), *Tools for Delivering on Green Growth,* OECD, Paris, available at www.oecd.org/greengrowth.

OECD/EEA Database on Instruments for Environmental Policy and Natural Resources Management, OECD /EEA, www.oecd.org/env/policies/database.

People's Republic of China (2011), "The Twelfth Five-Year Plan for National Economic and Social Development of The People's Republic of China", Approved at the Fourth Session of the 11th National People's Congress, March 14, 2011, People's Republic of China, Beijing.

Pindyck, R. S. (2007), *Uncertainty in Environmental Economics*, Oxford University Press on behalf of the Association of Environmental and Resource Economists, Oxford.

Pisu, M. (2010), "Tackling the Infrastructure Challenge in Indonesia", *OECD Economics Department Working Papers,* No. 809, OECD, Paris.

Porter, G. (2002), "Subsidies and the Environment: An Overview of the State of Knowledge", OECD Workshop on Environmentally Harmful Subsidies, OECD, 7 November 2002, OECD, Paris, available at www.oecd.org/dataoecd/41/26/35217152.pdf.

Schlegelmilch, K. (2007), "The Impact of the Ecological Tax Reform in Germany", in *Environmental Fiscal Reform in Developing, Emerging and Transition Economies: Progress & Prospects*, Documentation of the 2007 Special Workshop hosted by the Federal Ministry for Economic Cooperation and Development (BMZ) and the Deutsche Gesellschaft für Technische Zusammenarbeit (GTZ) GmbH, 2007 Global Conference on Environmental Taxation, 18-20 October, Munich, Germany, available at www.worldecotax.org/downloads/info/documentation_gtz-Workshop.pdf.

Sijm, J. P. M. (2002), "The Performance of Feed-in Tariffs to Promote Renewable Electricity in European Countries", ECN-C--02-083, European Competition Network, Brussels.

Small, K and K. van Dender (2007), "Long Run Trends in Transport Demand, Fuel Price Elasticities, and Implications of the Oil Outlook for Transport Policy", in *Oil Dependence: Is Transport Running Out of Affordable Fuel*, International Transport Forum/OECD, Paris, available at http://internationaltransportforum.org/jtrc/DiscussionPapers/DiscussionPaper16.pdf.

Steenblik, R. and J.A. Kim (2009), "Facilitating Trade in Selected Climate Change Mitigation Technologies in the Energy Supply, Buildings, and Industry Sectors", *OECD Trade and Environment Working Papers*, No. 2009/2, OECD, Paris.

Stern, N. (2009), *A Blueprint for a Safer Planet: How to Manage Climate Change and Create a New Era of Progress and Prosperity*, Bodley Head, London.

TEEB (2010), *The Economics of Ecosystems and Biodiversity: Mainstreaming the Economics of Nature: A Synthesis of the Approach, Conclusions and Recommendations of TEEB*, UNEP, Bonn.

Van Dender, K. and P. Crist (2010), "What does improved fuel economy cost consumers and taxpayers?", *International Transport Forum Discussion Paper* 2011-1, draft presented to ITF-KOTI Green Growth Workshop 25 November 2010, available at www.internationaltransportforum.org/Proceedings/GreenGrowth2010/VanDender.pdf.

Weitzman, M. L. (2001), "Gamma Discounting", *American Economic Review*, Vol. 91, pp. 260–271.

Weitzman, M. L. (2009), "On Modeling and Interpreting the Economics of Catastrophic Climate Change", *Review of Economics and Statistics,* Vol. 91, No. 1, MIT Press Journals, Massachusetts, pp. 1-19. available at http://nrs.harvard.edu/urn-3:HUL.InstRepos:3693423.

WHO (World Health Organisation) (2008), *Regional and Global Costs of Attaining the Water Supply and Sanitation Target (Target 10) of the MDGs*, WHO, Geneva.

WHO (2009), *Global Health Risks: Mortality and Burden of Diseases Attributable to Selected Major Risks*, WHO, Geneva.

World Bank (2005), *Integrating Environmental Considerations in Policy Formulation – Lessons from Policy-Based SEA Experience*, The World Bank, Washington DC.

Yermo, J. and C. Severinson (2010), "The Impact of the Financial Crisis on Defined Benefit Plans and the Need for Counter-Cyclical Funding Regulations", *OECD Working Papers on Finance, Insurance and Private Pensions*, No. 3, OECD, Paris.

Chapter 3. Promoting the transition towards green growth

Promoting a successful transition towards green growth means: (i) developing strategies for reform, (ii) facilitating adjustment in the labour market; (iii) accounting for concerns about distributional impacts on firms and households, especially those on low incomes, and (iv) promoting international co-operation.

Greening growth will see new green sectors and activities develop, in some cases displacing other activities. Labour market, skills, and education policies can help in smoothing the transition by focussing on:

- *Minimising skill bottlenecks and facilitating the acquisition of new skills required of workers in both new jobs and existing jobs.*

- *Ensuring that workers and firms are able to seize new opportunities arising from changes accompanying the greening of growth.*

- *Adapting other green growth policy, such as pollution pricing, in ways that can promote labour demand.*

Managing the distributional consequences of policies is crucial to reform success in terms of generating support and ensuring fair and positive outcomes:

- *Affected groups in society need to be part of the policy making process in the first instance. This process needs to be transparent and clearly articulate the justification for reform.*

- *Addressing the concerns of businesses, such as changes in competitiveness in the transition, ought to be addressed through multilateral policy co-ordination. Compensatory schemes can be justified but they come with their own costs.*

- *Negative impacts on poorer households need to be offset through well-targeted programmes, taking account of settings across the entire tax and transfer system.*

Creating a global architecture conducive to greener growth requires strengthened international co-operation for addressing environmental challenges, and for ensuring that all countries benefit from green growth and that domestic policy does not have negative consequences for others.

Reaching an agreement on the policies on which a green growth strategy should be based is only part of the picture. There remains a broader challenge of governance and political economy. In other words, it is necessary to understand how decisions are made, and in whose interest they are made – and how reform is promoted or obstructed and why.

Experience of reform in various domains can provide several general lessons (OECD, 2010a):

- *Crises can promote change.* The need for reform has to be identified clearly; otherwise stakeholders are unlikely to push for change or to agree on the priorities of any new policy. Crises are the most obvious sign that change is needed, but their influence on the desire to reform is not clear cut. It can also be argued that it is easier to reform when things are going well, and the transitional costs can be borne more easily. That said, waiting for an environmental crisis before acting is not an option, especially regarding ecosystems, whose nonlinear behaviour means that a slow, steady decline can abruptly accelerate beyond the point of no return.

- *Reform is often accompanied by calls for increased transparency in the availability, impacts and beneficiaries of government programmes.* Voter opposition to subsidies seen as having unacceptable economic costs and environmental effects makes subsidy reform less politically damaging for governments. Identifying who benefits from subsidies, and highlighting their relative "bargaining power", can provide a higher degree of transparency and thus can be a particularly powerful motivating force for change.

- *International factors may influence domestic reform.* For instance, foreign competition resulting from trade liberalisation incites domestic firms to seek reform of policies that put them at a disadvantage. International treaties or agreements can also lead to sectoral reforms, even in the face of domestic opposition.

- *Knowledge and influence are major factors in policy reform.* Poor practices may suit the immediate needs of a particular industry, but changing them can be hard because the industry knows the issues best and is skilful at exercising political influence on government decisions. This is however changing. The "information imbalance" is being redressed by knowledgeable, well-organised stakeholders with different objectives and considerable expertise.

- *Reform is a long-term process, before and after implementation.* Building support is essential to the success of the reform, and cannot be rushed, particularly where reform benefits specific groups only, while the costs are borne by the whole community. Pressure to wind back reforms can be significant, especially if particular interest groups have retained sufficient power or cohesiveness to influence the future course of policy. Withstanding such pressure can require significant political commitment and may need to be coupled with further measures to gain the support of remaining disaffected groups. Successful reform is generally not a one-off event, but is actually a process of continuous improvement over time that fine-tunes and adapts policies to evolving circumstances.

These issues can be seen in terms of international governance of a global commons that an increasing number of people are seeking to exploit, while the international structures that could manage this commons are inadequate. Governments administer the global commons, but they also defend their national interests.

Moreover, in designing and implementing green growth strategies governments need to find satisfactory compromises not only among conflicting objectives of different strands of society, but also within government itself. Green growth strategies cannot be implemented through a single type of policy, but getting the mix right requires a rare degree of co-ordination among ministries who may not be used to working together.

There are no tidy solutions to such political economy problems and implementation challenges, making a degree of political courage important. Past reform efforts suggest that the ingredients needed to make reform happen include (Llewellyn and de Serres, 2011) (Box 3.1):

- *Strong leadership.* Leaders need to gain the respect of constituencies, whether the public at large or cabinet colleagues. When an electorate is being asked to make sacrifices for a brighter future, trust and truth are important.

- *Strong institutions.* The ability, credibility, cohesion, and firmness of purpose of the political structure need to be emulated throughout the country's institutions (legislative, operational and informational). Treasuries and finance ministries in particular play pivotal roles.

- *Good economics is not necessarily bad politics.* OECD case studies cast doubt on the often-repeated claim that voters tend to punish reforming governments in the next election.

- *Employ change agents at all levels.* The communication process can be aided by "points of light" – people across society, ranging from business people to journalists to NGOs – who complement the top-down approach with more diverse, and more local, elaboration and support.

- *There is never a truly good time to implement reform.* OECD and IMF econometric evidence supports the view that the most promising time for reform is immediately after a recession or election. In reality however, economies often have to live with the consequences that emerge from sub-optimal policy sequencing.

To better understand the nature of economic change, three aspects of economic adjustment and policy reform associated with the transition to a greener model of growth, are considered: *i)* sectoral shifts and labour market implications; *ii)* how to assess and address competitiveness concerns; *iii)* how to deal with distributional impacts. Discussion also covers key issues that require increased co-operation and special attention to policy coherence at the international level.

Box 3.1.   The political economy of congestion charges: lessons learned

Traffic congestion, particularly road traffic, has costs that a green growth strategy could address. A United Kingdom Department for Transport white paper, Creating Growth, Cutting Carbon, (Department for Transport, 2011) estimates that excess delay is costing urban economies GBP 11 billion per annum and that carbon emissions impose a cost to society equivalent to up to GBP 4 billion per annum, while health costs are up to GBP 25 billion.

Economic evidence reviewed by the International Transport Forum (ITF, 2010) strengthens the case for using charges to tackle congestion. Lessons on the political economy of introducing charges successfully in London, Stockholm and Singapore and value pricing on some US highways may prove insightful for the development of green growth policies in other sectors. Reasons for the withdrawal of plans for national congestion charging systems in the UK and the Netherlands are equally relevant.

The main lessons can be summarised as follows:

- Congestion charging systems are only justifiable where congestion is severe, and even in this case significant efforts need to be put into ensuring that there is sufficient public awareness of the problem before charging is implemented.

- Congestion charges potentially raise substantial amounts of revenue, but the systems are costly to run as well, typically accounting for 10 to 30% of revenues.

- Revenue neutrality may appear to be a requirement for getting public and political support, but it reduces policy flexibility, and London shows that transparency and accountability in revenue use is at least as important for acceptance.

- Do not confuse objectives. There are cheaper ways to raise revenues and to protect the environment. Congestion charging is only applicable nationwide if congestion is a problem nationwide. If the primary objective is to make road taxes fairer, *e.g.* by charging foreign trucks on the same basis as domestic vehicles, or replacing a national tax that raises tax competition problems with neighbouring countries, more cost-effective alternatives are likely to be available.

- Do not phase in charges from a low base. This will fail to cut congestion, undermining support, and fuel fears that real motive for the charge is revenue raising.

- Ensuring acceptance may require giving up some of the benefits of a theoretically ideal system. Less-than-ideal systems such as simple pricing cordons and value pricing schemes can still be satisfactory.

- Rule-based systems for changing prices (*e.g.* maintaining pre-determined levels of speeds as in Singapore and the dynamic pricing applied to the I-15 freeway in San Diego) appear to be more popular than those requiring political discretion, *i.e.* periodic agreement by elected officials on charge levels/increases.

- Ancillary benefits, including reduced environmental impacts, can in some cases have an impact on how much to charge and should always be included in assessments, but they are not the principal goal of congestion charging mechanisms. Focusing on reducing CO_2 emissions when arguing for the introduction of congestion charges risks rejection.

Source: ITF (2010), "Implementing Congestion Charges" and Department for Transport (2011), "Creating Growth, Cutting Carbon: Making Sustainable Local Transport Happen".

Labour market implications

Greening growth will see new green sectors and activities develop and new skills required of workers in both new jobs and existing jobs that are re-engineered to become more environmentally friendly. Labour market and skills development policies can make an important contribution to greener growth. By minimising skill bottlenecks and preventing a rise in structural unemployment, these policies can make the transition to green growth quicker and more beneficial. By helping workers to move from contracting to expanding sectors, they can also assure a fairer sharing of adjustment costs arising from economic changes accompanying the greening of growth.

The job creation potential of investing in green activities

In the short run, the expansion of environmentally-friendly activities will create many jobs. The potential synergies between policies to promote a transition to green growth and policies to promote employment became clear during the recent global financial and economic crisis. Public investments in green activities played a significant role in the stimulus packages introduced to boost demand and the economic recovery. These investments offer a double dividend at a time of high unemployment, both jumpstarting job creation and accelerating the transition.

A number of governments have emphasised the sizeable impact on employment resulting from some of their green stimulus measures (OECD, 2010b). For example, the United States Council of Economic Advisers estimates that the USD 90 billion placed in clean energy investment in the US Recovery and Investment Act will save or create about 720 000 job-years by the end of 2012. Likewise, the KRW 50 trillion being invested as part of Korea's "Green New Deal" are expected to create 960 000 jobs from 2009 to 2012, including jobs in an environmentally-friendly transportation network, water management and river rehabilitation, clean energy, green information technologies, and waste-to-energy. France's stimulus package totalled USD 33.1 billion, 21% of which was designated for green measures, with an estimated net job creation of about 80 000-110 000 in the 2009-2010 period.

While synergies with short-run macro-stabilisation policy are welcome, the fundamental rationale for developing green activities and jobs is to contribute to sustainable growth in the long-run. It follows that policy packages that are intended to further both environmental and employment objectives need to be considered over a longer time horizon. For instance, an increasing number of studies put forward the large potential for job creation associated with the expansion of renewable energy generation and distribution. The recent report by UNEP, ILO, IOE and ITUC suggests that by 2030, given the increasing interest in energy alternatives, up to 20 million jobs could be created worldwide: 2.1 million jobs in wind energy production, 6.3 million in solar photovoltaic and 12 million in biofuels-related agriculture and industry (UNEP/ILO/IOE/ITUC, 2008). Likewise, the European Renewable Energy Council argues that the EU target for the share of renewables in total energy consumption to attain 20% in 2020 could create more than 2 million jobs (Renner, Ghani-Eneland and Chawla, 2009). The development of environment-related jobs extends well beyond most advanced economies: large developing countries have also undertaken large-scale initiatives (Box 3.1)

.

Box 3.2.   **Developing green activities and jobs: large-scale initiatives in China**

While the primary source of energy in China is coal, the development of renewable energy is a fundamental part of China's national strategy (ILO, 2011). Concerns about energy security, power capacity shortages, air pollution and climate change have all motivated a decision to place greater emphasis on raising energy efficiency while progressively switching to alternative technologies and fuels, including "clean coal" technologies, nuclear power, and renewable energy. As a result, the Chinese government took a number of policy initiatives: a renewable energy law was passed in 2005 and a plan was set in 2007, which put forward guiding principles, objectives, targets and measures for the development of renewable energy in China up to 2020.

During the period 2006-08, 12 detailed regulations for promoting renewable energy development were passed. And in 2008, total investment in renewable energy by China was ranked the highest in the world (Martinot and Junfeng, 2007). In addition, China's stimulus package included the largest green stimulus programme enacted by any country, accounting for almost 40% of the total USD 586 billion package (OECD, 2010b). Although there are no systematic surveys or other firm statistics indicating the number of people employed in the renewable sector, the Energy Research Institute and the Chinese Renewable Energy Industries Association have estimated that close to one million people in China are currently employed in the wind, solar PV, solar thermal, and biomass industries (UNEP/ILO/IOE/ITUC, 2008).

As Figure 3.1 shows, these various employment estimates are quite sensitive to the assumption regarding the expansion of renewable energy markets. They also rely on a number of assumptions regarding the employment content of the whole production, transformation and commercialisation process of renewable energy sources. Most importantly, these estimates represent the potential for *gross* job creation but do not take account of the fact that renewable energies will develop, to a considerable extent, at the expense of more polluting energy sources. In other words, green growth will involve new opportunities for workers, but also potential adjustment difficulties.

Figure 3.1.   **Employment projection in the renewable energy sector**

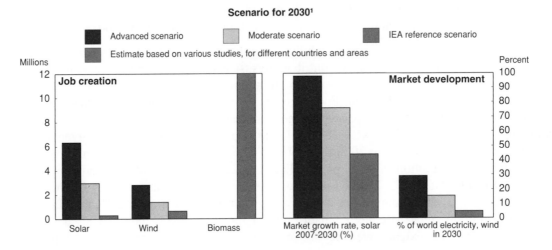

1. Estimates taken from the UNEP/ILO/IOE/ITUC report, based on EPIA and Greenpeace International (2007) p48 and GWEC and Greenpeace International (2006) p46.

Source: UNEP/ILO/IOE/ITUC (2008), *Green Jobs – Towards Decent Work in a Sustainable, Low-Carbon World.*

StatLink ⟶ http://dx.doi.org/10.1787/888932422249

In many cases, jobs potentially at risk are easier to identify than the new jobs that will be created. This is typically the case during periods of structural change. While green activities are still at a relatively early stage of their development and it is difficult to predict the large future sources of employment, data on major polluting sectors can provide a clue as to labour market impacts. Historical data on sectoral CO_2 emissions, for example, illustrate which are the most CO_2 intensive sectors and assessing their importance as employers.

Figure 3.2 suggests that the potential adjustment associated with greening growth is likely to be concentrated on a small portion of the total workforce. Indeed, while the most intensely-polluting industries account for a large share of total CO_2 emissions, they account for only a small share of total employment. In 2004, on average across OECD countries for which data are available, 82% of CO_2 emissions in the non-agricultural sector were generated by these industries, whereas they employed less than 8% of the total workforce.

Figure 3.2. Sectoral employment and CO_2 emission intensity

Unweighted average across 27 OECD countries, 2004[1]

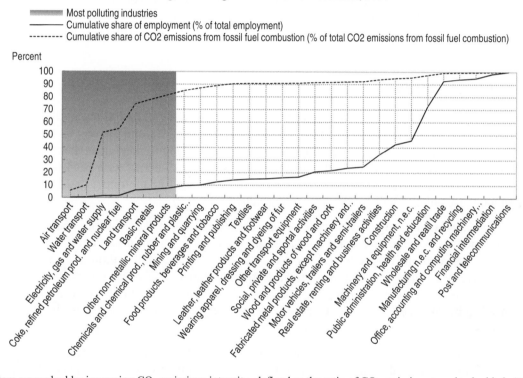

1. Sectors are ranked by increasing CO_2 emissions intensity, defined as the ratio of CO_2 emissions to valued added. At the level of disaggregation shown in the chart, seven sectors stand out as being the most polluting industries: three transport sectors, two energy producing sectors and two manufacturing sectors.

Source: EU-LFS, GTAP database, KLEMS database.

StatLink ⬛🖳 http://dx.doi.org/10.1787/888932422268

A number of detailed studies of the restructuring of the energy sector towards a cleaner energy-mix have concluded that *net* employment gains will result for energy-related activities.[1] This is because the renewable energy sector generates more jobs per megawatt of power installed, per unit of energy produced, and per dollar of investment, than the fossil fuel-based energy sector. Based on an in-depth analysis of 13 independent reports on the direct economic and employment impacts of the clean energy industry in Europe and the United States, Kammen, Kapadia and Fripp (2004) argue that increasing the share of renewable energy in the United States to 20% of consumption levels by 2020 could create more than 200 000 jobs (against less than 90 000 jobs in a scenario without renewables). Therefore, the winners would clearly outnumber the losers. In a similar vein, a study supported by the European Commission suggests that, summing up employment gains and losses in energy-related activities, nearly 1.4 million jobs could be created in Europe under the current policy –*i.e.* the 20% target for renewable energy by 2020 (Whiteley, M. *et al.*, 2004)

Overall, the bulk of studies examining the direct employment impact of greening the economy conclude that a shift away from conventional energy sources could lead to substantial net employment gains. As both the *direct* and *induced* labour requirements for the various energy technologies are reasonably well known, these studies provide reliable estimates of the employment content of a given energy-mix across the entire supply chain of production.[2] However, these are only the "first-round" net employment impacts. In most cases, these studies do not fully account for the "second-round" effects of a change in energy-mix: for instance, they usually do not model the policy drivers of this change and therefore, they do not fully capture the full macroeconomic impact of environmental policies. Kammen, Kapadia and Fripp (2004) indeed suggest that the balance between winners and losers from green growth depends on the state of the overall energy economy. When demand for energy is rising, as it is at present, there is more room for new energy suppliers to benefit. "*A recession, or economic or policy drivers of a shift from one technology to another – such as a shift away from coal that could result from a carbon tax – changes the equation dramatically.*"

The overall long-term employment effect

The overall employment impact of green growth policies is likely to be limited in the long run. The impact of these policies and of eco-innovation is likely to spread well beyond the sectors directly affected *via* indirect channels and can thus have pervasive effects across the entire labour market. Carbon pricing, for example, can create various structural adjustment pressures that interact with each other in complex ways, and a general equilibrium approach is required to capture all of the direct and indirect channels through which these policies will reshape labour markets.

By causing important changes in relative prices, carbon pricing will affect the composition of both final and intermediate demand and hence composition of labour demand. In particular, the relative price of energy and energy-intensive goods and services will increase. Eco-innovation is also likely to have important relative price effects, while also directly affecting labour input and job skill requirements in sectors making use of the new technologies. As a result, new jobs will be created while many existing jobs will need to be "greened" even as others will have to be reallocated from downsizing to expanding sectors or firms.

Barriers to industrial restructuring, such as poorly designed product market regulations or labour market institutions, could hinder the reallocation process and, ultimately, reduce the pace of employment growth. On the other hand, carbon pricing raises public revenue, which can be used to reduce other taxes. Revenue-neutral mitigation policies are sometimes advocated on the basis that they can generate a "double-dividend": the first dividend in terms of more effective environmental protection and the second reflecting the efficiency gains arising from the reduction in distortive taxes, such as labour taxes.

A growing number of economic modelling teams have developed and applied computable general equilibrium (CGE) models to analyse the economic impacts of climate change policies, including the impacts on labour markets. These models incorporate detailed specifications of the cleanest and most polluting technologies and industries into standard, multi-sectored CGEs, with the most ambitious models encompassing all regions in the global economy and international trade and investment flows. Because labour market policies and institutions vary widely across countries and interact in complex ways with policies in other markets, it remains a challenge to introduce a thorough representation of labour market in environmental CGE models that are already complex and not easily-tractable tools. Consequently, for the sake of simplicity, labour market imperfections are most often introduced through more or less *ad-hoc* forms of labour market rigidities. In order to clarify some of these implications for a transition toward green growth for labour markets, illustrative simulation exercises have been conducted looking at the implications of climate policies using the cross-country multi-sector general equilibrium OECD ENV-linkages model.[3]

The illustrative policy scenario applied in the modelling is an emission trading scheme (ETS) which, over the period 2013-2050, progressively reduces greenhouse gas (GHG) emissions in the OECD area as a whole by 50% in 2050 as compared to their 1990 levels.[4] The target is less stringent for non-OECD countries: emissions are reduced by 25% in 2050 as compared to what would be observed in these countries in the absence of mitigation efforts, under the so-called business-as-usual (BAU) scenario. Moreover, these countries do not participate in the OECD cap-and-trade scheme and, hence, undertake their emissions reductions independently.[5] This scenario does not account for any inefficiency in BAU or the welfare gains from avoiding damages from climate change.

Overall, the simulations indicate that this mitigation policy has a limited impact on economic growth and job creation. When permit revenues are redistributed in the form of uniform lump-sum transfers, carbon pricing tends to reduce slightly the pace of economic growth (Figure 3.3, Panel A). Mitigation costs increase with the degree of labour market imperfection, as structural distortions, reinforce the deadweight losses associated with a given carbon price. Yet, even in the worst-case scenario, under very strong labour market imperfections, economic growth is only slightly affected by the introduction of carbon permits: on average in the OECD area, real GDP increases by almost 41% over the period 2013-2030, as compared to 44% in the absence of mitigation actions. The resulting slowdown in job creation is more pronounced, but still not large.

Interestingly, the mitigation policy actually boosts employment growth when permit revenues are used to reduce taxation on labour (Figure 3.3, Panel C). For an intermediate degree of labour market rigidities, OECD employment would increase by 7.5% over the period 2013-2030, against 6.5% in absence of mitigation actions, and this, without any loss of purchasing power for workers.

Figure 3.3. Economic impact of mitigation policies, OECD average

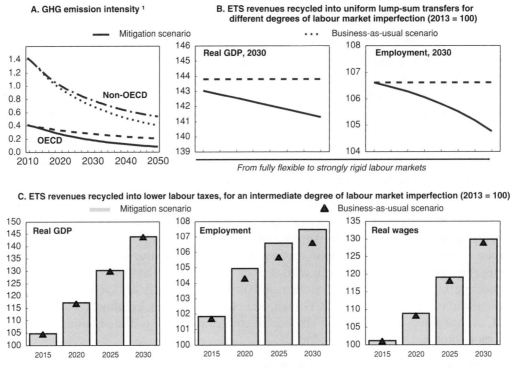

1. GHG emissions (Mt COeq) divided by real GDP (billions of 2007 USD).

Source: OECD ENV-linkages model.

StatLink ᴹᴵˢ᛫ *http://dx.doi.org/10.1787/888932422287*

These estimates illustrate how certain policy mixes can improve both environmental and labour market performance. They also show that both the quality of labour market institutions and the redistribution of permit revenues need to be jointly addressed in order to reap the full potential benefit of climate change policies in terms of job creation.

These conclusions are in line with many other studies analysing the employment impact of mitigation actions within the framework of a CGE model. For instance, a study by the European Commission estimates that the pace of employment growth in Europe could slow down slightly, should participating countries meet the EU's objectives on climate change and renewable energy for 2020 – 20% reduction of GHG emissions relative to 1990 levels and a target of 20% renewable energy by 2020 (Commission of European Communities, 2008). For selected European countries, Boeters and van Leeuwen (2010) show that a 20% reduction in energy use could slightly reduce unemployment, provided that energy taxes are used to reduce labour taxes. Babiker and Eckaus (2006) and Montgomery *et al.* (2009) obtain the same qualitative results for the United States, while also showing how labour market imperfections could increase mitigation costs.

In essence, green growth policies represent a timing issue: they require costs and economic adjustments in the short run to avoid larger costs and irreversible damage later. CGE models allow evaluating the transition costs, but over a longer time horizon, certain employment gains induced by mitigation policies (or job losses avoided) are not captured. Indeed, as innovation is intrinsically difficult to predict, the potential effects of environmental policies in stimulating the innovation of new green technologies is not fully captured. Likewise, most CGE models (including the ENV-linkages model) do not account for the potential economic damages from climate change and, hence, omits the economic benefits from mitigation policies that operate through reduced environmental disruption. And as underlined in Chapter 1, the damages from climate change may be large. Yet, innovation and climate change are slow processes, as illustrated in a recent report by UNEP showing that an increase in green investments would start producing positive employment outcomes in 2050 (UNEP, 2011).

Labour market and skills policies

Labour market and skills policies can play an important role within the overall policy framework for achieving green growth. Labour market policies should ensure that workers and firms are able to adjust quickly to changes brought about by greening growth, including by seizing new opportunities. By helping workers to move from contracting to expanding sectors, they can also help to assure a fairer sharing of adjustment costs occasioned by the transition.

The OECD Reassessed Jobs Strategy (RJS, OECD, 2006) provides a useful framework for identifying policies that can reconcile the vigorous process of "creative destruction" required to achieve green growth with a high level of employment and shared prosperity. One of the guiding principles of the *RJS*, which is especially relevant, is that a carefully designed package of labour market, social protection and skills development policies can assure that the labour market is both dynamic - continuously redeploying labour from declining to growing industries and firms - and inclusive. There are three policy areas that should be given priority in order to promote a *smooth* and *just* transition:

- A strong skill development system and active labour market programmes that facilitate a quick re-integration of jobseekers into employment are key supply-side policy elements for reinforcing the structural adaptive capacity of labour markets.

- On the demand side, moderate employment protection and strong product market competition are important supports for vigorous job creation as environmental policies and eco-innovation create new green competitive niches.

- Policies that increase the adaptive capacity of labour markets need to be combined with flanking measures, such as unemployment insurance and in-work benefits, which assure that dynamism is not achieved at the cost of excessive insecurity or inequality for workers and their families.

There is little historical experience with low-carbon and resource efficient growth from which lessons could be drawn. However, historical analogies to other recent drivers of deep structural changes in labour markets, such as the globalisation process and the information and communication technology (ICT) revolution, may provide qualitative insights into the potential challenges that lie ahead. An in-depth OECD study of structural adjustment policies in the context of deepening globalisation concluded that the RJS framework provided the necessary orientation for labour market policy to facilitate adjustment while also meeting social goals (OECD, 2005). It also suggests that general programmes should be relied upon as much as possible because specific programmes tend to increase administrative complexity and may lead to inequities. The same is likely to be true for meeting the structural adjustment challenge posed by the transition to green growth.

However, whereas the ICT and globalisation revolutions appear to have generally raised job skill requirements, it is not yet clear whether green growth will have a systematic impact on overall skill demand. Ramping up the pace of eco-innovation will tend to raise skill demands, at least for an extended period of time, provided that the expansion in green R&D does not imply an equal reduction in R&D for less environmentally friendly technologies. This suggests that a high priority should be placed on improving science, technology, engineering and maths (STEM) skills at all levels, as well as the broad range of technical, managerial and leadership skills that businesses will require to succeed in the green economy. The on-going development of an OECD Skills Strategy will thus represent a valuable support for an effective Green Growth Strategy.

Dedicated green education and training programmes will have an important role to play in helping workers to participate fully in the emerging green economy. Evidence from a number of countries suggests that skill shortages have already developed in certain sectors or occupations where green growth policies have created a need for new skills, or new combinations of familiar skills (Martinez-Fernandez, Hinojosa and Miranda, 2010). Energy-efficient construction and retrofitting, renewable energy, energy and resource efficiency and environmental services appear to be among the most affected sectors. For example, a report to the French government recently identified a number of emerging occupational specialties in the construction sector (*e.g.* energy auditors and solar panel installers), which are not well served by traditional training institutions and hence face potential recruitment bottlenecks (COE, 2010).

Other examples of skill shortages include difficulties reported by employers in recruiting skilled photovoltaic workers (Germany), design engineers for smart grids (the United Kingdom), installation and maintenance of solar electrical systems (Spain), and project managers with competencies in renewable energy in Denmark (CEDEFOP and ILO, 2010). However, it is difficult to assess how general and severe these green skill shortages are based on evidence from highly diverse case studies. Recent OECD work has shown that small and medium sized enterprises (SMEs) face particular challenges in upgrading or adapting their workers' skills to meet emerging job skill requirements associated with green growth (OECD, 2010c).

A recent OECD questionnaire on the green-related labour market programmes that governments have implemented or are planning to implement suggests that training and education programmes were a top priority; most countries regarding a well functioning training system as an essential element for green growth (Table 3.1). By contrast, job subsidies in private sector or direct job creation in the public sector are only rarely used as green employment measures.

Table 3.1 .   Green-related national programmes implemented by selected countries

	Job subsidies	Direct job creations	Education and training programmes		Job subsidies	Direct job creations	Education and training programmes
Australia	X		X	Japan			
Austria			X	Korea		X	X
Belgium	X	X	X	Mexico			
Canada			X	Netherlands			
Chile				Norway			
Czech Republic	X		X	Poland			
Denmark			X	Portugal			
Finland			X	Slovak Republic			
France			X	Slovenia			X
Germany				Spain		X	X
Greece	X		X	Sweden			
Hungary	X	X	X	Turkey			X
Israel				United States		X	X

Source: Chateau, J. and A. Saint-Martin (2011), "Employment Impacts of Climate Change Mitigation Policies in OECD: A General-Equilibrium Perspective", *OECD Environment Working Papers,* No. 32 (forthcoming).

It is noteworthy that slightly more than half of the responding countries have implemented specific green-related programmes at the national level, most of which were drafted in co-ordination with other ministries. In part, this may reflect the fact that policies to foster green growth are still at an early stage in a number of countries. And in more advanced countries, it may be the case that a green component has been added to a number a pre-existing labour programmes, although these programmes cannot be identified as specific green-related programmes. But this also reflects the fact that labour market and training policies in support of green growth are typically implemented at the local level, including by integrating them into comprehensive green development strategies.

Local administrations and communities can provide a key contribution to the strategies for human capital development as these must be integrated and matched to the economic reality on the ground (OECD, 2010d and 2008b). One key to success is to identify transferrable skills in the local workforce that is employed in declining firms and sectors that can be profitably employed in emerging greener sectors in the local economy. One interesting example is the Transversal Platform that has been launched by the south Alsace region in France.

Partnerships have also a key role to play in facilitating and managing the transition of local labour markets to the green economy. OECD work has found that partnerships act as catalysers of market opportunities and communicate the needs of the businesses and the sectors in general to the public sector, improving the development of policies and enhancing their effectiveness. The example of the region of Styria, in Austria, illustrates how effective public-private partnerships in a region can foster the development of the green economy and drive eco-innovation to the highest levels (OECD, 2010e). Active co-operation between management and workers' representatives and governments in accordance with national practices can also make an important contribution at the local, national and international levels.

Distributional impacts

Major policy reforms have frequently paid insufficient attention to distributional concerns. Claiming that policy changes will be "fiscally neutral", as in many climate-related initiatives in OECD countries, is insufficient. Details are needed. If the fiscal effects from green taxes, for example, are to be neutralised by reducing direct taxes on labour income, then clarity on planned changes is much more likely to assure constituencies that their interests are being taken into account. At the same time, the potential growth dividend also needs to be communicated. Consulting on how distributional impacts will be dealt with is a crucial part of policy communication. This includes taking careful account of how affected groups want to be compensated.

Managing the distributional consequences of policy is crucial to reform success in terms of generating support and ensuring fair and positive outcomes. Concerns about distributional impacts can be divided into potential competitiveness impacts on firms and welfare impacts on households.

Firms

Firms will claim unfair adverse impacts from policy change either in terms of increased costs vis-à-vis competitors or simply in terms of a change in the rules that undermines the ability to make a return on investment.

In most cases, such as pollutant pricing, cost increases are intended to drive a change in resource allocation in the economy; demand for pollutant-intensive goods will decline, prices may fall and so will returns on associated existing assets. While some firms will face costs, others will benefit. This is the objective of regulating environmental damages or resource use. The question is to what extent firms are exposed to unintended loss of competitiveness. Answering this requires understanding how the economy as a whole is likely to adjust in response to the introduction of such pricing.

The perspective of a firm or industry is often quite different to that of a policy maker charged with balancing the interests of society at large. Firms will focus on the upfront costs of environmental regulation in assessing their competitive position. From the policy maker's perspective this arithmetic is incomplete because it does not account for economy-wide adjustments in costs and prices. Furthermore, the principal economic driver of change in sectors facing cost increases is unlikely to be loss of competitiveness. An analysis of climate policy by the Australian government found, for example, that aluminium production was the only sector where a loss of competitiveness would cause output losses (Commonwealth of Australia, 2008). Some sectors that face upfront cost increases can even end up in an improved position as a result of domestic policy.

Resistance can be strong but needs to be kept in perspective. There will be those who have benefitted privately from activities that have imposed costs on wider society, such as unconstrained access to natural resources and inadequate restrictions on polluting activities. In this context, the costs of change need to be discounted, to the extent that change is not only necessary to facilitate increased welfare in societies, but is also a feature of economic growth.

At the extreme end of firms' concerns are examples of stranded assets, where investors are unable to recoup the costs of their investment due to a change in policy. Where firms can be identified and costs evaluated, lump sum transfers to compensate asset owners is the most efficient policy as it does not encourage continued pollution or unsustainable resource use, but this is often unpopular with the public. On the other hand, more popular policies which allow continued use of otherwise stranded assets, such as partial exemption of a plant or an industry, are likely to undermine the objective of reform. One is faced then with a choice between policy effectiveness and political feasibility.

The politics can be tough because the arithmetic of competitiveness is simple, easily expressed and readily digested by a wide audience of taxpayers and workers concerned about job losses or lower incomes. If a firm faces higher costs in its home country, it may struggle to compete, move offshore or lose its business to offshore companies and jobs will be lost. This resonates with many constituents and cannot be refuted in its entirety (Stephenson and Upton, 2009).

In addition, there will also be some concern that changes in investment and trade flows will cause a shift in polluting production to countries with less stringent regulations. This is known as the "pollution haven" effect. This is of particular concern in the case of global public goods, like the atmosphere, because it can undermine the achievement of the environmental objective which gives rise to the environmental regulation in the first place. In the context of climate change this is usually referred to as "carbon leakage".

It is unclear if the pollution haven effect actually exists in practice and studies which suggest it does tend to show that the effect is small. Indeed, recent work at the OECD (Kalamova and Johnstone, 2011) indicates that more stringent environmental policy can induce outward FDI flows, although the effect is small relative to other factors such as regulatory quality more generally. Moreover, the effect is non-linear, becoming negative when environmental policies in the recipient countries are too lax. This may be due to the adverse "signalling" effect of weak environmental policies for potential investors.

The existence of pollution haven effects can be hard to argue against on the face of it. Other things being equal, production will migrate to where regulatory costs are lowest. The result is a chilling effect with respect to the introduction of stringent policies. The simplicity of this message gives it traction, even though in reality the effects of environmental policies on production and investment decisions pale in comparison to factors such as access to and cost of financing, exchange rate risk, certainty of supply, general regulatory or tax environment, quality of institutions and infrastructure, and proximity to input and output markets.

There are, however, sector-specific cases where environmental regulation is a potentially large part of costs and therefore an important factor in firms' location and production decisions. In these cases, there is a much higher prospect of pollution haven effects. To the extent that these are related to global public goods this is *a priori* justification for considering ways of managing this risk (see *Tools for Delivering on Green Growth*: Table 12).

Policy options that are often considered include:

- Exemption of at-risk firms or industries.

- Financial compensation through offsetting tax changes, rebates, including free allocation of pollution permits.

- Making tax adjustments at the border so that imports face the same costs as domestic production or domestic production is not disadvantaged in export markets.

The most controversial policy option tends to be the use of tax adjustments at the border because it imposes costs on other countries' exports, would have very limited benefits in terms of reducing leakage, and could exacerbate any contractions in production among energy intensive industries because it raises input costs.

Historically, exemptions tend to be most frequently used and these can be very costly. For instance, exempting energy-intensive industries from the application of a carbon tax or a cap-and-trade scheme could raise the global cost of achieving a given emission-reduction target by as much as 50% (OECD, 2009). Moreover, exemptions and other policies that are selective in application require policy makers to determine which firms should be supported and which should not. There is no precise or objective way to do this and thus the door is open to rent-seekers.

There is also evidence of cases where exemptions can be shown to have been unnecessary while also leading to substantial negative environmental impacts.

Compensatory measures, such as free allocation of pollution permits, are likely to be much less costly than exemption, but information and transaction costs can be high and difficult choices need to be made about how such compensation is delivered. One approach is to grandfather any compensation to existing firms. This helps to address the concerns of the principal opponents of policy, but it also introduces risks around windfall gains to those firms and potentially creates barriers to entry of new and potentially more efficient firms.

Another approach is to provide offsetting compensation based on firm output. Because production is effectively subsidised, firms' competitiveness is in principle preserved (Reinaud, 2008). Unlike grandfathered compensation, there should be little effect on sector-wide product prices, and new entrants are treated the same as existing facilities (Smith, 2008). For the system to operate effectively, there should be a single output upon which the refunding can be based and each plant's output should be small enough relative to the total output to form a competitive market (OECD, 2010f).

With refunds, polluters are less likely to protest against an environmental charge, and it becomes politically easier to set a high enough charge to generate substantial environmental improvements. Differential incentives that are inherent to the structure of the refund may even create a natural constituency in support of the refund (Smith, 2008).

Although these compensatory schemes can be useful in defusing competitiveness concerns, they have also been shown to reduce rates of innovation among firms (OECD, 2010g).

Moreover, any benefits from these schemes will decline with the increase in the number of countries pursuing green growth policies. In this regard, multilateral policy co-ordination is one alternative to unilateral measures. It is also critical in cases where collective action is needed to secure the objectives of environmental policies. Recent work in the area of long-range transboundary pollutants has shown that the transfer of knowledge and technologies is greater amongst signatories following adherence to a Multilateral Environmental Agreement (OECD, 2011a).

However, multilateral co-ordination will not remove all concerns about competitiveness and pollution havens. Differences in national circumstances and domestic policy choices, whether in the name of green growth or otherwise, mean that policies will continue to differ and firms are unlikely to ever compete on an entirely level playing field.

Households

In terms of households, invariably there are concerns about the potentially regressive nature of taxes and the income effects associated with the reform of environmentally-harmful subsidies. Particularly in the case of taxes on water and energy use for heating, such concerns have impeded implementation in many countries or have led to modifications in the tax design in order to reduce the burden on low-income households, which spend a higher proportion of their income on utilities. While progressivity is a consideration, it is the progressivity of the entire tax/social system that is important.

Therefore, such concerns are best addressed by means such as lower personal income taxes, tax credits and increased social benefits rather than by reducing or exempting low-income households from the environmentally-related tax, and thus removing their incentives to use water or energy more efficiently. OECD country experiences show that strong communications and credible institutional arrangements, such as a green tax commission and multi-stakeholder dialogue, can help to overcome some of the concerns regarding green tax reform.[6]

In principle, if any regressive relationship between an environmentally-related tax and income is a tight one, then changing income taxation or income-related benefits would be a good way of compensating poorer losers. However, in practice there may be a looser relationship, so it may be harder to target compensation exactly. The details of the inclusion of measures to compensate politically sensitive losers in packages will always depend much on the national institutional context, but as long as it is accepted that all consumers will have to bear the economic cost of achieving a cleaner environment relative to their income, a package can be constructed that improves overall welfare while reducing income inequalities.

Concerns of households about distributional effects are likely to be particularly strong in the case of taxes to reduce emissions of greenhouse gases where there is no visible direct benefit to domestic households (unlike, *e.g.* SO_x emissions or congestion charges), and taxes are likely to be seen as unrequited. This holds true also with respect to the global public good benefits associated with biodiversity. It is important to note however, that distributional impacts of existing biodiversity policy may already be skewed against the poor. This is because most biodiversity is located in developing countries. Costs of biodiversity conservation and sustainable use are normally borne locally (hence by poorer countries) while the benefits often accrue at local, as well as regional and global scale (see also OECD, 2008b).

Similarly, attempted reforms to energy subsidies have faced public resistance, sometimes leading to their reversal (Box 3.3). Energy subsidies are typically in place for social considerations to make available a basic need at a price affordable to the poor. They affect real household incomes both directly and indirectly. The direct effect is the gain in disposable income due to lower prices paid by households for consumption of fuel products. The indirect effect is seen in the lower prices paid by households for other goods and services stemming from the lower cost for fuel-based inputs of production.

In many cases, however, the benefits of fuel subsidies tend to accrue mainly to high-income groups while their cost falls on the whole tax-paying population. For example, an IMF study (Coady *et al.*, 2006) found that when direct and indirect benefits are considered, the bottom 40% of the population in Bolivia, Ghana, Jordan, Mali, and Sri Lanka receive only 15-25% of fuel subsidies. In India, LPG and kerosene subsidies, prior to energy sector restructuring, were mostly used by higher expenditure groups in urban areas, and much of the subsidy was wasted because about half of the subsidised kerosene supplies is diverted and never reaches consumers (Gangopadhyay, Ramaswami and Wadhwa, 2005). These findings suggest that the subsidies are very ineffective in improving the welfare of the poor.

While simply removing energy subsidies entails the risk of an increase in poverty, there is an opportunity for the associated savings to be targeted more effectively to lead to overall positive effects on poverty alleviation. The effects of energy subsidy reform on poverty will depend on the extent to which low-income households are compensated for the rise in prices and on the efficiency of such compensation policy.

Resulting spare resources could be efficiently used to introduce compensating measures that support the real incomes of the poorest households in more direct and effective ways. International experience shows that transition support must be well targeted, coherent with underlying broader policy settings of economies and carefully planned. Among all the available social policy tools, cash transfers present advantages. They distort markets and incentives less than other programmes, they can be easily targeted and their cost is usually known with certainty. When properly implemented, most of the cash transfer funds can be channelled to the poor. Increasing subsidised energy prices would also facilitate the financing of additional spending on health, education and infrastructure (de Mello, 2010), which are crucial to raising living standards in the longer term.

Box 3.3.   Political economy challenges – the case of energy subsidy reform in India

In the context of its commitment as a member of the G-20 to reduce fossil fuel subsidies, India has recently made welcome progress in reducing some energy subsidies. In the 2011 Budget the government announced that it would start to move away from the current system of subsidies on kerosene, LPG and fertilisers. Its objective is to move, from March 2012, to a direct cash subsidy to people with incomes below the poverty line.

The economic and environmental benefits of phasing out energy subsidies in India are far from trivial. For example, modelling simulations indicate that the gradual removal of fossil fuel subsidies would increase real income by around 2.5% in 2050 as a result of improvements in resource allocation across sectors. In addition, India's greenhouse gas emissions would also be over 15% lower relative to the status quo by 2050 (OECD, 2010b).

Such reform is not easy given the vested interests of those who benefit from the status quo (OECD, 2007). A high degree of transparency will be required for building support for reform and challenging those against it. This requires good information on the magnitude of subsidies, their economic and environmental impacts as well as their distributional consequences. This should provide the basis for a strong communication programme to increase awareness of the benefits of subsidy reform. Building the case for reform also requires strong political leadership and broad support across government departments, including finance, industry, energy, environment, rural development and agriculture.

Well-targeted compensation to address distributional concerns is also a key element of successful subsidy reform. Although low-income households only benefit from a small proportion of India's energy subsidies, they are likely to be disproportionately affected by their removal as they spend a higher percentage of their household income on energy. Also, effective strategies that encourage the poor to switch to cleaner and more efficient fuels can bring considerable heath benefits (Wilkinson *et al.*, 2009). Accordingly, a move to market-based pricing for petroleum products must be carefully designed to not restrict energy access and increase energy poverty. As foreseen in the 2011 Budget, support to the poor should be directly targeted and allow the recipients to purchase petroleum products at any retail outlet. A support system along these lines would not interfere with market pricing and thereby remove the myriad arbitrage opportunities that have been abused for so long in India. By being much better targeted, direct transfers to the poor would vastly reduce the extent of petroleum product subsidies.

Subsidy reforms are also more likely to be successful when they are done as part of a package of broader structural reforms. In India, the reform and phase-out of energy subsidies needs to be accompanied by *e.g.* subsidy reform in other areas, including reform of fertiliser subsidies and removal of cross-subsidies in electricity markets, in conjunction with subsidy rationalisation in the coal and rail transport sectors.

Source: OECD (2011), OECD Economic Surveys: India (forthcoming).

International co-operation for green growth

Global challenges require co-operation on a global scale in order to deliver public goods (climate change mitigation, biodiversity) or protect the global commons (the environment, fisheries). International co-operation is necessary because: *a*) no single country can successfully address the problems alone; *b*) the costs and benefits of action may accrue to different countries, and individual countries may not be willing to bear the costs of addressing global challenges if they cannot appropriate the benefits; and *c*) uncoordinated efforts of many countries to address global challenges are likely to be more costly and less successful than co-ordinated, co-operative efforts. Examples of recent international initiatives on green growth by the OECD and partner organisations are summarised in Box 3.4.

Creating a global architecture which is conducive to green growth will require further strengthening of arrangements for managing access to the global commons, increased co-operation in the field of science and technology, provision of finance to support action by developing countries, and facilitating the diffusion of clean technologies. Increased effort to boost global trade and investment flows would also help to underpin sustained growth and access to clean technologies. This could include resolution of the current round of WTO trade negotiations and increasing environmental dimensions in regional trading agreements. At the same time, there is a need for increasing vigilance around the potential spill-over effects of domestic policy measures on trade and investment and the potential for incoherent policy which undermines development prospects in low income countries.

Managing global public goods is a critical area for co-ordinated international action. A key pressure point in this regard is balancing the benefits of biodiversity, which accrue globally, with the opportunity costs of maintaining biodiversity, which are strongest in developing countries. The global ecosystem services that these environmental assets can provide accrue to the whole world, and have highest marginal value in the better off countries; however, the opportunity costs in foregone economic development of maintaining them may be borne mostly by the poor population groups in the countries themselves, leading to difficult policy choices. For example, choosing not to bring more land under cultivation because of the high environmental costs associated with agriculture will be difficult for a country with high levels of rural poverty. Systems to pay developing countries for ecosystem services can help to capture some of the global value associated with these services, and increase the economic benefits to accruing from maintaining the natural assets. These could play a pivotal role in building support for – and ensuring the political feasibility of – green growth strategies.

Climate change is a global challenge that also requires global co-operation because of fundamental co-ordination and incentive failures and the fact that poor countries will be most severely affected while capacity to address climate change tends to lie outside of these countries. Poor people in developing countries are disproportionately vulnerable to environmental degradation as their livelihoods are frequently dependent on agriculture and the use of other natural resources.

In yet other areas, the shared nature of common resources will require international co-operation to ensure against over-exploitation of some natural resources. Rapid depletion of catch fisheries and the existence of policies which encourage over-fishing are an example of one area of concern for which there appears little hope of remedy outside co-ordinated action in the multilateral sphere.

While the international community has agreed a number of targets or plans to address these challenges, sizeable gaps remain with respect to the action being taken on the ground to achieve them. For example, there is widespread acceptance that countries have failed to meet the 2010 target to achieve a significant reduction in the rate of biodiversity loss globally that was agreed in 2002 by Parties to the United Nations Convention on Biological Diversity. Similarly, the climate change mitigation pledges countries have made following the Cancun COP16 conference on climate change are insufficient to reduce emissions so as to limit the increase in global average temperature below 2 degrees Celsius.

There are many important complementarities between moves to green the economy and poverty reduction. Natural capital comprises as much as 25% of the total per capita wealth in low-income countries, and as such the sustainable and productive use of this natural capital can be a central part of green growth in these countries and ensuring sustainable livelihoods for poor people. That being said, mechanisms will be needed to ensure that the technologies to facilitate their actions are developed and available, that the financial and capacity development support is provided, and that other policies - such as those that affect trade and investment decisions - are mutually supportive of development and environmental objectives, rather than conflicting. For instance, the Nagoya Protocol includes some mechanisms to secure a fair and equitable sharing of benefits from genetic resources.

Science and technology

International co-operation in science and technology has a long tradition, but the current challenges require more concerted approaches to accelerate technology development and diffusion. The use of new innovative mechanisms for financing innovation (*e.g.* securitisation, risk sharing and forward commitments) and for enhancing technology transfer (*e.g.* voluntary patent pools and other collaborative mechanisms for leveraging intellectual property) will be particularly important. The search for solutions to global challenges would benefit from a closer involvement of the developing world in science and technology co-operation, and from the building up of research and technology capacity in these countries. As was indicated in Chapter 2, absorptive capacity in the receiving country is a critical factor in ensuring successful technology transfer.

An example of an important institutional framework that has potential to promote the transfer of green technologies from developed to developing countries is the Clean Development Mechanism (CDM). There are two objectives of the CDM, (1) to assist developing countries in achieving sustainable development and in contributing to the ultimate objective of the United Nations Framework Convention on Climate Change (UNFCC) and (2) to assist parties included in Annex I in achieving compliance with their qualified emissions limitation and reduction commitments (greenhouse gas emission caps) under the Kyoto Protocol. The second objective is achieved by allowing Annex I countries to meet part of their caps using certified emissions reduction (CER) credits through CDM emission reductions projects in developing countries. Most CDM activity has been in richer countries[7], particularly China. A recent review of whether the technologies transferred via the CDM correspond to the needs of developing countries (Kim and Popp, 2011) suggests that there are noticeable and interesting differences between the technologies demanded by low and middle-income countries. Some technologies for which demand in low-income countries is likely to be high such as solar energy for remote locations, improved cook stoves, and efficient lighting appear "neglected" by the CDM. Nonetheless, a review of costs for these technologies suggests that they could be cost-effective for developing countries.

In Cancun, climate change negotiators agreed to establish a Technology Mechanism, including creating a Technology Executive Committee and a Climate Technology Centre and Network. The Technology Executive Committee is in charge of providing an overview of technological needs and analysis of various policy and technical issues related to the development and transfer of technology for mitigation and adaptation activities, as well as to catalyse the development and use of technology road maps or action plans to fight climate change. The Climate Technology Centre and Network will facilitate a network of national, regional, sectoral and international technology initiatives and organisations. These initiatives will help promote international co-operation and may lead to global economic and environmental benefits.

Development co-operation

Development co-operation has been an early mover in relation to environmental sustainability and has already contributed significantly to greening growth in developing countries. ODA targeted to environmental purposes amounted to USD 26 billion in 2009, a 45 % increase from 2007 (Figure 3.4). The OECD Development Assistance Committee (DAC) is also tracking the bilateral aid that supports the objectives of the three Rio Conventions: UN Framework Convention on Climate Change (UNFCCC), UN Convention on Biological Diversity (CBD), and the UN Convention on Combating Desertification (UN CCD). Sustainable natural resource management is a priority focus of many bilateral aid programmes and Environmental Impact Assessments are a normal requirement of all significant aid-funded infrastructure projects in developing countries.

Figure 3.4.   Aid targeting environmental challenges

As classified by the Rio Conventions, USD million [1]

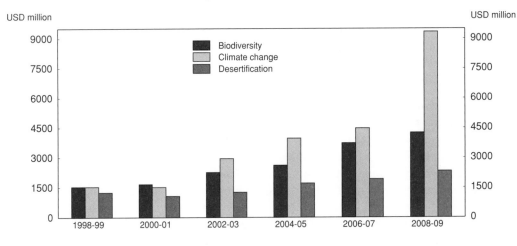

1. Members of the OECD's Development Assistance Committee (DAC), two-year averages, commitments, constant 2008 prices.

Source: OECD-DAC: CRS Aid Activity database.

StatLink 📊 *http://dx.doi.org/10.1787/888932422306*

ODA can continue to play an important role in areas where private sector flows are scarce – such as essential infrastructure and human and institutional capacity development – to create enabling conditions for green growth. For example, more than USD 2 billion by OECD donors were allocated to railway transport to reduce greenhouse gas emission from the transport sector in 2009, and ODA for renewable energies recently surpassed that of ODA for non-renewable energies. These public investments play an instrumental role to avoid lock-in to carbon-intensive infrastructures and in many cases to mobilise private investment in these areas.

ODA is also often used to provide technical assistance to developing country governments and to facilitate dialogue between international experts and partner country governments. Such capacity development will be critical in the context of poor countries, enabling them to identify and implement a green growth strategy that suits their particular circumstances, to tackle environmental challenges and to maximise their efforts toward sustainable development. This aspect of international co-operation efforts is front and centre in climate change negotiations, as a way to scale-up mitigation efforts to achieve the desired stabilisation levels of greenhouse gas emissions, as well as to enhance adaptation actions aimed at reducing vulnerability and building resilience in developing countries.

ODA's contribution to green growth in developing countries can be further strengthened by ensuring that climate proofing and disaster risk reduction approaches are mainstreamed in aid-funded public investments. Similarly aid for poverty reduction needs to promote livelihoods that are more secure and resilient to climate change and environmental degradation. It should aim to assist with major developmental shifts, such as urbanisation, where the scale of investment needed and the associated planning needs make this a particular important front for advancing a green growth.

Developed countries have also been providing financing to support international environmental objectives through multilateral development banks, as well as a range of specific funds. The Global Environment Facility (GEF) provides grants to developing countries and economies in transition for projects related to biodiversity, climate change, international waters, land degradation, the ozone layer, and persistent organic pollutants. To date, the GEF has allocated USD 9.2 billion in funding. A number of Funds have been established under the UNFCCC to support action to tackle climate change in developing countries, including the Adaptation Fund, a Fund to support action in Least Developed Countries, and most recently the Green Climate Fund that was established through the Cancun Agreements in December 2010.

In addition to bilateral and multilateral finance, governments have an important role to play in establishing the policy frameworks that can help facilitate private investment in low-carbon, climate-resilient and resource-efficient infrastructure, and to use the scarce public resources available to better leverage or crowd-in this private finance, as discussed in Chapter 2. While the use of international emissions trading and climate offsets, as initially embodied in the Kyoto Protocol, poses some challenges such as in terms of ensuring additionality of action, such mechanisms hold considerable potential in terms of international co-operation. They provide a natural mechanism for financial transfers, allowing for a clear separation between where emission cuts take place (where it is cheapest to do so) and who bears the cost. In this regard, countries pursuing or operating emission trading schemes on a domestic or regional basis should do so with a view to linking schemes and leveraging them as a financial transfer mechanism.

Trade and investment

Increased global trade is a key driver of growth and an important avenue for greening growth trajectories. Similarly, international investment is a vital source of finance and a powerful vector of innovation and technology transfer as countries seek to promote green growth.

Policy makers should pursue the benefits from co-ordinated action and a degree of policy harmonisation which allows for continued gains from trade and differential use of the global commons according to different levels of development and comparative advantages. In this regard, successful completion of multilateral trade talks could play an important role in greening growth, especially to the extent that ambitious outcomes are achieved in environmental goods and services trade and commitments are made to reduce harmful subsidies. Similarly, regional trade arrangements are showing increasing promise as a way to lower barriers to trade in environmental goods and services and as a means of improving policy co-ordination and capacity building.

There is often a desire to see local industry benefit from business opportunities that arise from policy changes. Governments may seek to build local manufacturing capacity to support deployment of renewable electricity technologies or provide support to local vehicle manufacturers to make greener vehicles. There may be a justification for governments to support the deployment of particular technologies, but that support should not be based on domestic preferences. Long-term growth is fuelled by gains from trade, whether within domestic or international markets. Including environmental considerations in the pursuit of long-term growth does not change this calculus. The desire to see new jobs created needs to be balanced against the gains to producers and consumers in having access to new technologies and competitively priced products and services. Demands for government purchasing to be directed locally need to be balanced against the need to get value for taxpayers' money.

For example, investment incentives to automotive firms can be beneficial if those firms are pursuing novel technologies. But there is not so much benefit if investment incentives simply help firms to retool with existing technology at the expense of the market share of firms who went in that direction on their own. A number of stimulus programmes introduced in the wake of the recent economic crisis included such investment incentives. As time-limited stimulus measures they may have been appropriate, but they are not good candidates for longer term green growth measures.

Preferences to domestic industry, whether explicit or otherwise, can be counter-productive especially if there is a risk of counter-measures from other countries. In the extreme, this can result in tax competition which favours specific firms at considerable fiscal expense. In other cases, it can hamper the execution of public projects when local content requirements create bottlenecks in supply chains.

Even in the absence of explicit domestic preference, support for green industry can have undesirable effects. In some cases, such as markets for solar photovoltaic panels, "large differences in support levels across countries have created market distortions, diverting supplies to the countries that provide the heaviest subsidies and raising prices for consumers elsewhere" (Steenblik, 2009).

Demand side policies also need to be carefully scrutinised for undue negative effects on trade. For example, in recent years there has been considerable growth in the use of labels that indicate the environmental impacts of products. While labels that are based on international standards can contribute to the mutual supportiveness between environment and trade, label information can be very sensitive to a large number of assumptions about the impact of production methods on the environment. This introduces the prospect of bias towards local information and production practices. At worst, the close involvement of local producers could lead to "industry capture" of the process with bias towards accounting for information which favours domestic producers and thus an increase in barriers to trade (Vitalis, 2002).

The OECD-hosted Freedom of Investment (FOI) Roundtable recently issued a communication on "Harnessing Freedom of Investment for Green Growth" which aims at making governments' environmental and investment policy goals mutually supportive (Annex 1). Governments are encouraged to continue to monitor their investment treaty practices with regard to environmental goals. It is also important that new environmental measures observe key international law principles such as non-discrimination (creating a level playing field for domestic and international investors). This process is most effective and efficient if it is integrated into policy design at an early stage. International investment arbitration is assuming a growing role in resolving disputes involving environmental issues, placing special responsibility on the investment policy community to ensure the integrity and competence of arbitral tribunals and to improve their transparency.

The FOI Roundtable communication also addresses the concern, expressed by some countries, that investment could be affected if the green growth policy agenda were captured by protectionist interests. However, none of the 42 countries that report regularly to the Roundtable about investment measures have reported overt discrimination against non-resident or foreign investors in relation to environmental policy. Neither have participating countries reported serious concerns about such measures by other countries. Nonetheless, continued vigilance is encouraged, and the Roundtable will continue to monitor investment measures to ensure that they are not used as disguised protectionism. Environmental policy measures that appear to be neutral may potentially involve de facto discrimination or create barriers to trade which constrain development. Some environment-related state aids (such as grants, loan guarantees or capital injections for individual firms), may potentially pose risks to competition.

Policy coherence for development

Policy coherence is also needed to ensure that all countries benefit from green growth and domestic policy does not have negative consequences for others. Green growth in major economies, especially OECD and emerging economies, is likely to affect smaller and less developed countries. The nature of these impacts will be vary on a case by case basis, influenced by factors such as country's trade pattern, natural resource endowments, carbon intensity and sources of energy, as well as environmental climates (Ellis *et al.*, 2010).

Developed and emerging countries should take into account how their policies for green growth may affect developing countries. The European Union took such considerations into account in its fishery access agreements with Mauritania. In 2006, the EU increased its financial contribution to EUR 86 million per year and included in the agreement specific provisions for developing the local fisheries sector and improving the control and surveillance of fisheries activities, thereby helping to conserve the resource (OECD/Economic Community of West African States, 2008 and Agritrade, 2007).

Box 3.4. Selected international initiatives on green growth

Alongside national plans and with a view to also contribute to the 2012 Rio+20 Conference, recent efforts to foster green growth entail a growing number of international initiatives by a range of organisations including the UN (*e.g.* ESCAP, UNEP, FAO) and the World Bank. The UNEP-led Green Economy Initiative (GEI) was launched in 2008 and brings together the activities of over 20 UN agencies under the overarching objective to promote investment in green(er) sectors. Since 2010, the GEI has been providing advisory services to a number of governments, with an active presence in fifteen countries. In February 2011, UNEP launched its report *Green Economy: Pathways to Sustainable Development and Poverty Eradication* (UNEP, 2011), which asserts that a green economy is not only relevant to more developed economies but can be a key catalyst for growth and poverty eradication in developing countries as well.

As part of the efforts to support countries on assessing progress towards green growth, the OECD and UNEP are working closely together and with other organisations, such as the United Nations Statistics Division (UNSD), other UN agencies, the World Bank, EUROSTAT, and the European Environment Agency (EEA), to develop a common set of core indicators for green economy.

Amongst some of the key international initiatives exploring the implications of green growth at the sectoral level is the FAO's project on Greening the Economy with Agriculture. The project aims to add to the definition and implementation of the green economy in the context of sustainable development, food security and poverty alleviation through the mobilisation of the food and agriculture sector. FAO seeks to team up with international partners on this initiative, including collaboration with the OECD. A joint FAO-OECD international expert meeting will be held in September 2011. In addition, the IEA and the OECD are developing a joint report on green growth in the energy sector which will be launched in June 2011.

More broadly, in March 2011 the World Bank called on governments and development agencies to join a new global knowledge platform on green growth. The platform, being developed jointly by the World Bank, UNEP and the OECD, aims to bring together proponents of sustainable development to promote and implement green growth policies by exchanging knowledge, information, and experience. The three organisations are also joining their efforts to provide co-ordinated contributions to Rio+20, which will mark a key milestone for promoting a global green economic transformation.

Other emerging institutions, notably the Global Green Growth Institute (GGGI), are playing an increasingly important role in the creation of a global architecture conducive to driving greener growth. Promoting a strong partnership and knowledge-sharing between a diverse group of international and regional organisations as well as governments, the GGGI aims to support the creation and diffusion of green growth that integrates objectives for poverty reduction, opportunity creation, and social development, with objectives for environmental sustainability, climate resilience, and energy security.

Notes

[1] Considerable work has been done on the employment impact of mitigation actions in the energy sector. See work by Kammen, Kapadia and Fripp (2004), Pearce and Stilwell (2008), and IEA (2009).

[2] For example, the task of installing wind turbines is a direct job, whereas manufacturing the steel that is used to build the wind turbine is an induced job.

[3] The OECD ENV-Linkages model is a recursive dynamic general equilibrium model, documented in detail in Burniaux, Chateau and Dellink (2010). It has been used extensively for several OECD publications, notably the *Environmental Outlook to 2030* (OECD, 2008a) and *The Economics of Climate Change Mitigation* (OECD, 2009b). While in the core version of the ENV-Linkages model, aggregate employment is treated as an exogenous variable, the model has been enhanced so that the employment impact of climate change policies can be analysed (see OECD, 2011a and Chateau and Saint-Martin, 2011).

[4] For Mexico, it is assumed that emissions are reduced by 50% in 2050 as compared to 2005 levels.

[5] This mitigation scenario is purely illustrative and not intended as a policy recommendation.

[6] One example of a forum for multi-stakeholder dialogue is the *Grenelle de l'environnement* in France www.legrenelle-environnement.fr.

[7] Perhaps this is because the match between Annex I technologies and host country needs are greater there.

References

Agritrade (2009), "ACP-EU Fisheries Relations", *Executive Brief*, December 2009, Agritrade, Wageningen available at http://agritrade.cta.int/en/fisheries/acp_eu_fisheries_relations/executive_brief.

Babiker, M. and R. Eckaus (2006), "Unemployment Effects of Climate Policy", MIT Joint Program on the Science and Policy of Global Change, *Report* No. 137, Massachusetts Institute of Technology, Massachusetts.

Boeters, S. and N. van Leeuwen (2010), "A Labour Market Extension for WordScan – Modelling Labour Supply, Wage Bargaining and Unemployment in a CGE framework", *CPB Document,* No. 201, CPB Netherlands Bureau for Economic Policy Analysis, The Hague.

Burniaux, J.-M, J. Chateau and R. Dellink (2010), "An Overview of the OECD ENV-Linkages Model 2010", *Background Report*, OECD, Paris.

CEDEFOP (European Centre for the Development of Professional Training) and ILO (2010), *Skills for Green Jobs: European Synthesis Report*, Publications Office of the European Union, Luxembourg.

Chateau, J. and A. Saint-Martin (2011), "Employment Impacts of Climate Change Mitigation Policies in OECD: A General-Equilibrium Perspective", *OECD Environment Working Papers,* No. 32, OECD, Paris (forthcoming).

Coady, D., M. El-Said, R. Gillingham, K. Kpodar, P. Menas and D. Newhouse (2006), "The Magnitude and Distribution of Fuel Subsidies: Evidence from Bolivia, Ghana, Jordan, Mali, and Sri Lanka", *IMF Working Papers,* WP/06/247, International Monetary Fund, Washington DC.

COE (Conseil d'orientation pour l'emploi) (2010), *Croissance verte et emploi* (Green Growth and Employment), COE (Conseil d'orientation pour l'emploi : Policy Board for Employment), Paris.

Commission of the European Communities (2008), "Package of Implementation Measures for the EU's Objectives on Climate Change and Renewable Energy for 2020", a *Commission Staff Working Document*, Commission of the European Communities, Brussels.

Commonwealth of Australia (2008), "Australia's Low Pollution Future: The Economics of Climate Change", Summary Report, Commonwealth of Australia, Canberra.

De Mello, L. (2010), "Enhancing the Effectiveness of Social Policies in Indonesia", *OECD Economics Department Working Papers*, No. 810, OECD, Paris.

Department for Transport (2011), "Creating Growth, Cutting Carbon: Making Sustainable Local Transport Happen", *White Paper*, Department for Transport, London.

Ellis, K., N. Cantore, J. Keane, L. Peskett, D. Brown and D. Willem te Velde (2010), "Growth in a Carbon Constrained Global Economy", Overseas Development Institute, London, available at www.dfid.gov.uk/R4D/PDF/Outputs/ClimateChange/60742-4984.pdf.

EPIA (European Photovoltaic Industry Association) and Greenpeace International (2007), *Solar Generation IV – 2007*, EPIA, Brussels and Greenpeace International, Amsterdam.

Gangopadhyay, S., B. Ramaswami and W. Wadhwa (2005), "Reducing Subsidies on Household Fuels in India: How Will it Affect the Poor?" *Energy Policy*, Vol. 33, No. 18, Elsevier, Amsterdam, pp. 2326-2336.

GWEC (Global Wind Energy Council) and Greenpeace International (2006), *Global Wind Energy Outlook 2006,* GWEC, Brussels, and Greenpeace International, Amsterdam.

IEA (2009), "Ensuring Green Growth in a Time of Crisis; The Role of Energy Technology", OECD/IEA, Paris, available at www.iea.org/Papers/2009/ensuring_green_growth.pdf.

ILO (International Labour Organisation) (2011), "Promoting Decent Work in a Green Economy", ILO Background Note to *Towards a Green Economy: Pathways to Sustainable Development and Poverty Eradication* (UNEP, 2011), ILO, Geneva.

ITF (2010), "Implementing Congestion Charges", *Discussion Paper*, No. 2010-12 ITF, OECD, Paris, summary available at www.internationaltransportforum.org/jtrc/DiscussionPapers/DP201012.pdf.

Kalamova, M. and N. Johnstone (2011), "Environmental Policy Stringency and Foreign Direct Investment", *OECD Environment Working Papers* (forthcoming).

Kammen, D., K. Kapadia and M. Fripp (2004), "Putting Renewables to Work: How Many Jobs Can the Clean Energy Industry Generate?", *RAEL Report*, University of California, Berkeley.

Kim J.E. and D. Popp (2011), "The Clean Development Mechanism and Neglected Environmental Technologies", Draft Report to the OECD Environment Directorate (unpublished).

Llewellyn, J. and A. de Serres (2011), "The Political Economy of Climate Change Mitigation Policies: How to Build a Constituency to Address Global Warming?", *OECD Economics* Department *Working Papers* (forthcoming).

Martinez-Fernandez, C., C. Hinojosa and G. Miranda (2010), "Greening Jobs and Skills: Labour Market Implications of Addressing Climate Change", *OECD Local Economic and Employment Development (LEED) Working Papers*, No. 2010/2, OECD, Paris.

Martinot, E. and L. Junfeng (2007), *Powering China's Development: The Role of Renewable Energy*, Worldwatch Report, Worldwatch Institute, Washington DC.

Montgomery, D., R. Baron, P. Bernstein, S. J. Bloomberg, K. Ditzel, A. E. Smith and S. D. Tuladhar (2009), "Impact on the Economy of the American Clean Energy and Security Act of 2009 (H.R.2454)", *CRA International Report* prepared for National Black Chamber of Commerce, Washington DC.

OECD (2005), *Trade and Structural Adjustment: Embracing Globalisation*, OECD, Paris.

OECD (2006), *Boosting Jobs and Incomes: Policy Lessons from Reassessing the OECD Jobs Strategy*, OECD, Paris.

OECD (2007), "Subsidy Reform and Sustainable Development: Political Economy Aspects", *OECD Sustainable Development Studies*, Paris.

OECD (2008a), *Environmental Outlook to 2030*, OECD, Paris.

OECD (2008b), *People and Biodiversity Policies: Impacts, Issues and Strategies for Policy Action*, OECD, Paris.

OECD (2009), *The Economics of Climate Change Mitigation: Policies and Options for Global Action beyond 2012*, OECD, Paris.

OECD (2010a), *Making Reform Happen: Lessons from OECD Countries*, OECD, Paris.

OECD (2010b), *Green Growth Strategy Interim Report: Implementing our Commitment for a Sustainable Future*, Document prepared for the Meeting of the OECD Council at Ministerial Level, 27-28 May 2010, OECD, Paris.

OECD (2010c), "Leveraging training and skill development activities in SMEs – Cross-country analysis of the TSME survey", paper by the Local Economic and Employment Development Programme, OECD, Paris.

OECD (2010d), *Entrepreneurship, SMEs and Innovation*, OECD, Paris.

OECD (2010e), "Climate Change, Employment and Local Development: Preliminary Findings", paper by the Local Economic and Employment Development Programme, OECD, Paris.

OECD (2010f), *Eco-Innovation in Industry: Enabling Green Growth*, OECD, Paris.

OECD (2010g), *Taxation, Innovation and the Environment*, OECD, Paris.

OECD (2011a), *The Invention and Transfer of Environmental Technologies*, OECD, Paris.

OECD (2011b), *OECD Economic Surveys: India* (forthcoming).

OECD (2011c), *Tools for Delivering on Green Growth*, OECD, Paris, available at www.oecd.org/greengrowth.

OECD/Economic Community of West African States (2008), *Fishing for Coherence in West Africa: Policy Coherence in the Fisheries Sector in Seven West African Countries, The Development Dimension*, OECD, Paris.

Pearce, A. and F. Stilwell (2008), "Green-Collar Jobs: Employment Impacts of Climate Change Policies", *Journal of Australian Political Economy*, No. 62, University of Sydney, Sydney, pp. 120-138.

Reinaud, J. (2008), "Issues behind Competitiveness and Carbon Leakage: Focus on Heavy Industry," *IEA Information Paper*, OECD/IEA, Paris.

Renner, M., M. Ghani-Eneland and A. Chawla (2009), *Low-Carbon Jobs for Europe: Current Opportunities and Future Prospects*, World Wide Fund for Nature, Brussels.

Smith, S. (2008), "Environmentally Related Taxes and Tradable Permit Systems in Practice", OECD, Paris.

Steenblik, R. (2007), "Biofuels – At What Cost? Government Support for Ethanol and Biodiesel in Selected OECD Countries", Global Subsidies Initiative of the International Institute for Sustainable Development, Geneva.

Steenblik, R. (2009), "Green Growth, Protectionism, and the Crisis", Chapter 14 in Evenett, S.J., B.M. Hoekman and O. Cattaneo (eds.), *Effective Crisis Response and Openness: Implications for the Trading System*, World Bank, Washington DC, pp. 249-262.

Stephenson, J. and S. Upton (2009), "Competitiveness, Leakage, and Border Adjustment: Climate Policy Distractions?" Background Paper for the 23rd OECD Round Table on Sustainable Development, 22-23 July, 2009, OECD, Paris.

UNEP (2011), *Towards a Green Economy: Pathways to Sustainable Development and Poverty Eradication*, UNEP, New York, available at www.unep.org/greeneconomy/.

UNEP, ILO, IOE, ITUC (2008), *Green Jobs – Towards Decent Work in a Sustainable, Low-Carbon World*, report produced by Worldwatch Institute and commissioned by UNEP, ILO, IOE, ITUC, Nairobi, available at www.unep.org/labour_environment/features/greenjobs.asp.

Vitalis, V. (2002), "Private Voluntary Eco-labels: Trade Distorting, Discriminatory and Environmentally Disappointing", Round Table on Sustainable Development, OECD, Paris.

Whiteley, M., A. Zervos, M. Timmer and F. Butera (2004), "MITRE Project Overview Report: Meeting the Targets and putting Renewable Energies to Work", European Commission DG TREN Altener project, Brussels, available at http://mitre.energyprojects.net/.

Wilkinson, P., K.R. Smith, M. Davies, H. Adair, B.G. Armstrong, M. Barrett, N. Bruce, A. Haines, I. Hamilton, T. Oreszczyn, I, Ridley, C. Tonne, Z. Chalabi (2009), "Public Health Benefits of Strategies to Reduce Greenhouse-Gas Emissions: Household Energy", *The Lancet*, Vol. 374, No. 9705, Elsevier, London, pp. 1917-29.

Chapter 4. Measuring progress towards green growth

Monitoring progress towards green growth requires indicators based on internationally comparable data. These need to be embedded in a conceptual framework and selected according to well-specified criteria. Ultimately, they need to be capable of sending clear messages which speak to policy makers and the public at large.

Four areas have been chosen to capture the main features of green growth:

- ***Environmental and resource productivity,** to capture the need for efficient use of natural capital and aspects of production which are rarely quantified in economic models and accounting frameworks.*

- ***Economic and environmental assets,** to reflect the fact that a declining asset base presents risks to growth and because sustained growth requires the asset base to be kept intact.*

- ***Environmental quality of life,** capturing the direct impacts of the environment on people's lives, through e.g. access to water or the damaging effects of air pollution.*

- ***Economic opportunities and policy responses,** which can be used to help discern the effectiveness of policy in delivering green growth and where the effects are most marked.*

A first assessment across some of these measures shows that while there are significant differences between countries, the growth of GDP tends to outstrip growth in environmental inputs into the production system. However, improved environmental productivity is not necessarily accompanied by absolute decreases in environmental pressure or the sustainable use of some natural assets.

An important measurement agenda remains, including the selection of a small set of headline indicators. The present set comprises about 25 indicators, not all of them measurable today.

Integrating economic and environmental policies requires a matching framework, definitions and comparable data to measure progress towards green growth. For convenience, the definition used in this report is repeated here: *green growth is about fostering economic growth and development while ensuring that natural assets continue to provide the resources and environmental services on which our well-being relies. It is also about fostering investment and innovation which will underpin sustained growth and give rise to new economic opportunities.* Green growth has thus several dimensions, "greening growth" and harnessing new growth possibilities from environmental considerations. By its very nature, such a process is not easily captured by a single indicator, and a small set of measures will be needed. Also, the ambition of the indicators is pragmatic: green growth indicators are seen as markers or milestones on a path of greening growth and of seizing new economic opportunities.

The set of green growth indicators listed below and elaborated fully in the companion document on indicators constitutes work in progress. It is a starting point rather than a final list and will be further elaborated as new data become available and as concepts evolve. Indeed, a central conclusion from the work on indicators is the measurement agenda that is drawn up at the end of the chapter. It provides the way forward towards addressing the most pressing data development needs in the area. Further discussions will be needed in the implementation of the measurement agenda.

Any quest for measuring green growth has to start with a measure for "growth" and the first candidate in this context is gross domestic product, GDP. GDP is and remains a central metric of economic growth. But it needs to be used for the purpose for which it was conceived, namely measuring market and government production and the associated economic activity. In the context of green growth indicators, GDP is a useful measure when it comes, for example, to comparing emissions from production with a country's production. GDP also enters as the appropriate metric to gauge the importance of the environmental goods and services sector.

However, GDP largely reflects market valuations of economic goods and services and consequently does not reflect environmental externalities associated with production and consumption. Also, as a gross measure, GDP takes no account of depreciation, depletion and degradation of assets. In a context of measuring societal progress and well-being, GDP will be insufficient as the only measure of growth. For instance, GDP generally overlooks the contribution of natural assets to well-being, for instance through human health. Even as a measure of living standards or material well-being, GDP is a less-than-perfect indicator. Here, household consumption or real net income measures are preferred: one reason is that distributional information can be attached to measures of consumption or income. Ultimately, it may also be possible to value depletion and degradation of natural assets in a measure of net income. A green growth strategy therefore has to target several measures of economic growth: GDP for production, consumption or real income and possibly their distribution among households for material well-being. Except for a small set of measures that relate to the environmental quality of life, no attempt is made in the context of the green growth strategy to draw a more comprehensive picture of well-being. This is left to other complementary work on measuring progress undertaken by the OECD.

Measurement framework

A natural starting point for defining green growth indicators is the sphere of production where economic inputs are transformed into economic outputs (goods and services) (Figure 4.1). A direct source of economic growth is therefore the growth of inputs, in particular labour, produced capital such as machines, and intermediate inputs that are used up in production such as steel in the automobile industry. But production also uses services from natural assets, either in the form of natural resource inputs into production (these may be non-renewable such as minerals extracted from the ground or renewable such as fish stocks) or in the form of disposal services where the natural environment provides services as a sink for pollutants and residuals emitted during production[1]. Services from natural assets are rarely quantified in economic models and accounting frameworks and yet they are central to examining the greening of growth. A first set of indicators is therefore environmental and resource productivity, representing the volume of output per unit of services from natural assets. Rising environmental and resource productivity would appear to be a necessary condition for green growth.

Changes in environmental and resource productivity can reflect several effects, including substitution processes between natural assets and other inputs, shifts in industry composition or overall, "multi-factor" productivity change. In a first instance, it will not be able to empirically distinguish between these effects but such work figures prominently on the measurement agenda. Some care must therefore be taken when interpreting partial productivity measures although the caveats relating to environmental productivity are not different from those relating for instance to labour productivity. But environmental and resource productivity indicators would appear useful nonetheless. The choice of specific indicators in this area was governed by the idea of capturing key aspects of a low-carbon, resource-efficient economy. As these indicators deal with the production side of the economy, growth has been captured by GDP.

It is also of interest to introduce the notion of demand-based environmental services, *i.e.* those flows of environmental services or emissions that are induced by domestic final demand but not necessarily by domestic production. In the case of emissions, this "footprint" approach tracks the emissions embodied in imports, adds them to direct emissions from domestic production and subtracts the emission contents of exports. The resulting figure informs about the direct and indirect contents of environmental services in domestic final demand – essentially consumption of households, governments and investment.

Figure 4.1.   Framework for green growth indicators

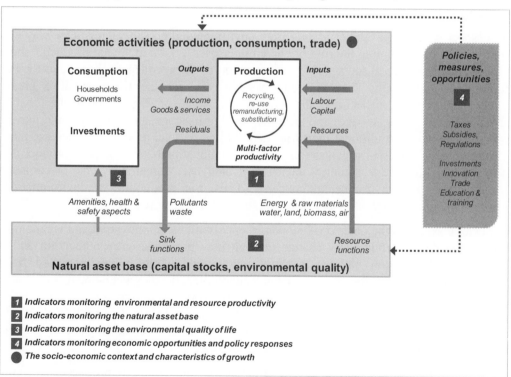

The production perspective outlined above is not sufficient to monitor the transition towards green growth. For sustained growth, the asset base has to be kept intact. One reason is that a declining asset base constitutes a risk to growth and such risks should be avoided. "Asset base" should be understood in a comprehensive way, encompassing produced as well as non-produced assets, and including in particular environmental assets and natural resources. Broader concepts[2] such as sustainable development would also include human capital or social capital. For purposes of the green growth strategy, however, the focus will remain on economic and natural assets. Loosely speaking, "keeping the asset base intact" implies that net investment is positive – more needs to be added to the asset base in the form of investment or natural regeneration than is subtracted though depreciation or depletion[3]. Whether a particular growth path of consumption or income can be sustained depends also on expected rates of multi-factor productivity change[4], thus adding to the central role that innovation and technical change play in considerations about green growth. A major question is how easily one type of asset can be substituted for another asset, *i.e.*, if the decline in one type of asset can be made up for by an increase in another type of asset. In a world of perfect measurement and perfect markets, this information should be contained in asset prices, reflecting society's preferences and vision of the future. Absent such prices for most assets, measurement has to start with monitoring the physical evolution of natural assets and this constitutes the second type of green growth indicators. Over time, measurement efforts should be undertaken to advance on the valuation of (net investment) in at least some important natural assets. This has been reflected in the measurement agenda.

Considerations about keeping society's asset base intact relate direct to one dimension of the quality of life that is relevant for the work at hand, namely the direct impact of the environmental on people. Environmental outcomes are important determinants of health status and well-being more generally. They provide an example where production and income growth may not be accompanied by a rise in overall well-being[5]. For instance, air pollution, in particular exposure to particulate matter, is much higher in some of the emerging economies than across the OECD countries. In addition, a larger share of the population lives under medium to severe water stress, while low levels of wastewater treatment and pollution contribute to the incidence of waterborne and preventable diseases. The third group of green growth indicators thus deals with the environmental quality of life.

A fourth aspect is the opportunities arising from environmental considerations. One way of framing relevant indicators is by examining the role of "green industries", trade in "green products" and creation of "green jobs". While widely discussed, closer inspection of these concepts shows that they are often difficult to pin down statistically. There is a more basic question whether the potential for green growth is adequately captured by measuring the output and jobs of those companies that produce environmentally related goods, services and technologies. For instance, an economy could move towards a low carbon growth path if traditional industries (say mining or steel production) increase their energy efficiency through new modes of organisation – process innovation – or if there is product innovation that leads to products that are less energy intensive in their use, triggered by cost or competitiveness considerations rather than environmental concerns. Thus, the production of environmental goods, services and technologies is only *one* aspect of the potential for green growth.

Another central aspect in the context of economic opportunities is innovation and technology. These are drivers of multi-factor productivity change through new products, entrepreneurship and business models, and new consumption patterns. General innovation has to be distinguished from green innovation. The latter mainly relates to research and technological development aimed at innovations that can address environmental challenges. A trade-off arises from the perspective of constructing green growth indicators. Focusing on green innovation indicators does not do justice to the full importance of innovation but general indicators of innovation are not very helpful in monitoring society's responses to the green growth challenge. The work at hand covers both aspects.

Clear and stable market signals are key to affecting the behaviour of producers and consumers. "Getting the prices right" has to be one of the major policy concerns when producers and consumers cause negative externalities to the environment through their economic activity. Several of the policy response indicators relate to environmental taxes and transfers. Regulatory instruments should not be forgotten as a tool to reduce negative effects on the environment. Constructing indicators of regulation is tricky, however, as the information is often of a qualitative nature and hard to compare across countries. No results are shown here but the point has been marked in the measurement agenda.

Overall, then the measurement framework explores four inter-related groups of indicators: *i)* indicators reflecting the environmental efficiency of production and consumption; *ii)* indicators of the natural asset base; *iii)* indicators monitoring the environmental quality of life, and *iv)* indicators describing policy responses and economic opportunities.

Emerging messages

The first set of indicators brought together provides a wealth of information and a few general messages arise already at this point. The first relates to environmental productivity: while there are significant differences between countries, the picture that emerges in many environmental areas is one of rising environmental and resource productivity. For example, as shown in Figure 4.2 for the case of CO2 emissions, the growth rates of GDP and other measures of output tend to outstrip the growth rates of environmental inputs into the production system or the need for sink services provided by the environment to human activity.

Rising environmental productivity is a necessary but not sufficient condition for pursuing less environmentally harmful economic growth. For this, rising productivity should be accompanied by absolute declines in environmental services in those areas where there is unsustainable use of environmental assets. A second message that arises here is that although such absolute "decoupling" has occurred in some countries and in some areas, it is less prevalent than relative decoupling. Cases of absolute decoupling in OECD countries are, for example, found for emissions of acidifying substances and related trans-boundary air pollution.

Further, trends in rising environmental and resource productivity can partly be explained by displacement effects. Substitution of domestic production by imports can lead to domestic decoupling without there being decoupling at the global level. For example, the decrease in the amount of CO_2 emissions per unit of GDP in many OECD countries is at least partly explained by imports of goods with a relatively high carbon footprint from other countries, notably China.

Figure 4.2.   Decoupling trends – CO_2 and GHG emissions

Index 1990=100

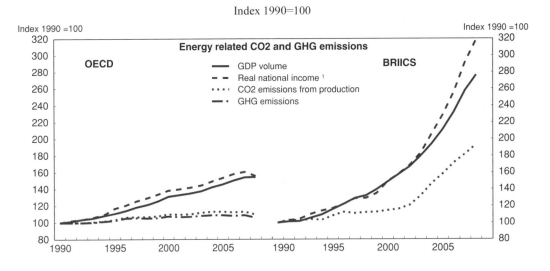

1.   Real net national income for OECD, and real gross national income for BRIICS.

Source: OECD-IEA, UNFCCC.

StatLink 🔗 http://dx.doi.org/10.1787/888932422325

While the demand perspective is important in the debate on global environmental issues, the policy implications of the demand-based indicator are less clear. The links between trade, economic growth and the environment are complex and any argument has to be weighed against the benefits of trade in enabling growth and development. Thus, at this time, the empirical findings should be taken for what they are, an attempt to measure economic phenomena but not a policy conclusion how to deal with them.

Green growth cannot be discussed without attempting to measure the economic importance of the production of environmentally-related goods, services and technology. A look at the evidence[6] about the size of production activities of goods and services produced for "green" purposes leads to several conclusions.

- As a share of GDP or employment, environmentally-related goods and services industries is comparatively small (Figure 4.3). For instance, a study by the United States Department of Commerce (2010) finds that green products and services comprised between 1% and 2% of the total private business economy in 2007. This must be put in perspective, however. As a share of imports and exports, the OECD has found larger numbers and several studies[7] foresee a significant growth potential, in particular in the emerging economies. Also, even small sectors can have large growth contributions when they grow quickly.

- Much depends on how exactly "green" industries are defined. A standard exists at the European level and guidance is emerging in at the broader international level through the UN System of Environmental Economic Accounting (SEEA), but remains to be implemented.

- More generally, whereas the production of green goods, services and technology are of interest, they only tell part of the story. Much of the environmental and many of the growth effects are likely to be associated with greening the economy as a whole, independent of whether particular products are put to environmental use. Quantifying these effects is much more difficult and in the realm of modelling rather than simple indicator development.

Figure 4.3.   Employment shares of some environmental goods and services industries[1]

As a percentage of total economy [2]

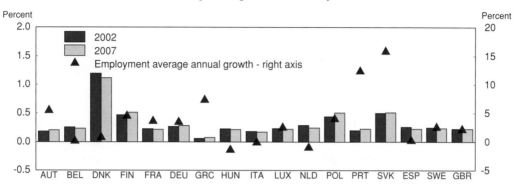

1. Environmental industries are Recycling (ISIC37), Collection, purification and distribution of water (ISIC41) and Sewage and refuse disposal, sanitation and similar activities (ISIC90).

2. Total economy is defined as ISIC sectors 10 to 74 excluding 65 to 67.

Source: OECD (2011), *Entrepreneurship at a Glance 2010* (forthcoming).

StatLink 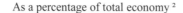 http://dx.doi.org/10.1787/888932422344

Remaining measurement issues

The need for a consistent accounting framework

Measurement issues constrain the full and timely production of green growth indicators. Some issues are located at the conceptual level and many issues are of an empirical nature. By their very nature, green growth indicators have to combine economic and environmental information, and do so in a consistent way. While there is a substantive amount of economic and also environmental data, it is often difficult to combine them due to differences in classifications, terminology or timeliness. A first and crucial ingredient of the measurement agenda is thus to develop and populate a consistent environment-economy accounting framework. The new and forthcoming System of Environmental and Economic Accounting (SEEA) provides such a framework. Measurement efforts should be placed within this framework so as to maximise consistency and international comparability.

Specific areas

Apart from the general usefulness of integrated statistics, the present preliminary set of green growth indicators revealed several important gaps in the information base. These areas should form part of a green growth measurement agenda, to be implemented over the coming years. In particular,

- There are significant gaps in environmental-economic data at the industry level. Improving the data situation would for example help quantifying the effects of industry structures on international comparisons of economy-wide indicators. More sectoral information is also useful from a policy perspective if policy tools are industry-specific.

- There is a need to develop and improve the physical data for key stocks and flows of natural assets. A prominent example is information on land and land use changes. Land is not only a major asset in a country's balance sheet, land use change is also a meaningful indicator for the interaction between economic activity and biodiversity. Another example is non-energy mineral resources that often constitute critical inputs into production.

- Better physical data also helps improving material flow analyses that could be undertaken at a more granular level and be extended to demand-based measures, akin to the methodology used to assess the CO_2 contents of domestic final demand. Such work would fit with the measurement agenda on material flows and resource productivity spelled out by OECD Ministers in 2008.

- Information on biodiversity remains scarce. Further efforts are needed in particular with regards to species and ecosystem diversity, and species abundance, and the genetic diversity of domesticated plant crops and livestock and their wild relatives (which is the basis for innovation and adaptation in the agricultural sector).

- Efforts should also be directed at developing monetary values for (changes in) key stocks and flows of natural assets. In particular, valuation of investment and depreciation (in the case of produced assets) and natural growth and depletion or degradation (in the case of non-produced natural assets) should be advanced. Guidance on measurement approaches is being provided by the forthcoming SEEA and by UN-ECE/OECD/Eurostat (2009). Such valuations, even if incomplete and imperfect are required:

  - to extend traditional growth accounting to include natural assets, thereby deriving new measures of multi-factor productivity growth;

  - to develop more comprehensive balance sheets;

  - to take first steps towards measures of real income that have been adjusted for natural growth and depletion of natural assets.

- The information base on how environmental concerns trigger innovation in companies remains limited. Regular innovation surveys and exploitation of other microdata sets could help advancing relevant knowledge about the drivers and impediments to innovation in conjunction with businesses' environmental and resource efficiency.

- Government consumption accounts for a sizeable part of economic activity and demand. In its production and public procurement activities, governments have important leverages to pursue green growth objectives. Yet there is hardly any quantitative or qualitative information on procurement that would permit tracking greening growth in this area.

- Environmentally related policy tools are more easily framed in indicators when they are economic instruments such as taxes or subsidies. The construction of indicators is more complicated when it comes to regulatory instruments. Thought should be given how indicators on economic instruments can be complemented by indicators on environmental regulation to balance the picture of international comparisons of policy responses.

- Measuring the effects of environmental conditions on quality of life and on life satisfaction is not an easy task. It requires improvements in both objective and subjective measures of the quality of life, in particular:

  - Environmentally induced health problems and related costs; and

– Public perceptions of the environmental quality of life that provide insight into citizens' preferences and sense of well-being.

Headline indicators

The present set comprises about twenty indicators, not all of them are measurable today (Table 4.1). The multi-dimensional nature of green growth requires a sufficient number of indicators to do justice to the various aspects of the issue at hand. But a large dashboard also carries the danger of losing a clear message that speaks to policy makers and helps communication with the media and with citizens.

One way of addressing this issue is to construct a composite indicator. The advantages of ease of communication and concise presentation of a composite number must, however be weighed against the problem of choosing units and weights required for aggregation across very different elements. Although there are ways to accommodate some of the issues involved in aggregation (Nardo *et al.*, 2005), the present work does not pursue this avenue. Rather, it is proposed that a small set of "headline" indicators be selected that are able to track central elements of the green growth concept and that are representative of a broader set of green growth issues. This is a task that still lies ahead and requires broad consultation and discussion because, inevitably, opinions on the most salient set of indicators will vary among stakeholders. The OECD stands ready to take this task forward.

Table 4.1.   Overview of proposed indicator groups and topics covered

Main indicator groups	Topics covered
The socio-economic context and characteristics of growth	
Economic growth, productivity and competitiveness	Economic growth and structure Productivity and trade Inflation and commodity prices
Labour markets, education and income	Labour markets (employment / unemployment) Socio-demographic patterns Income and education
Environmental and resource productivity	
Carbon and energy productivity	1. CO_2 productivity (demand-based, production-based) 2. Energy productivity
Resource productivity	3. Material productivity (demand-based, production-based) Non-energy materials, waste materials, nutrients) 4. Water productivity
Multi-factor productivity	5. Multi-factor productivity including environmental services
Natural asset base	
Renewable stocks	6. Freshwater resources 7. Forest resources 8. Fish resources
Non-renewable stocks	9. Mineral resources
Biodiversity and ecosystems	10. Land resources 11. Soil resources 12. Wildlife resources
Environmental quality of life	
Environmental health and risks Environmental services and amenities	13. Environmentally induced health problems and related costs 14. Exposure to natural or industrial risks and related economic losses 15. Access to sewage treatment and drinking water
Economic opportunities and policy responses	
Technology and innovation	16. R&D of importance to GG 17. Patents of importance to GG 18. Environment related innovation
Environmental goods and services	19. Production of environmental goods and services
International financial flows	20. International financial flows of importance to GG
Prices and transfers	21. Environmentally related taxation 22. Energy pricing 23. Water pricing and cost recovery
Training & skill development Regulations & management approaches	*Indicators to be developed:*

Notes

[1] Alternatively, emissions could be treated as negative or undesirable outputs rather than as inputs of environmental services. This is a matter of convenience and labelling but measurement implications are unchanged.

[2] See in particular the work by UN-ECE/OECD/Eurostat (2009). The World Bank's *Genuine Savings Indicator* rests on the same foundations: a necessary condition for sustainability is that net savings are non-negative.

[3] For a rigorous formulation of this condition and an overview of the academic literature, see Heal and Kriström (2005).

[4] The discounted cumulative flow of expected rates of multi-factor productivity change can be considered an intangible asset. See Nordhaus (1995), Weitzman (1997) and Hulten and Schreyer (2010) for theoretical discussions and some back-of-the envelope estimates.

[5] Conceptually, and in terms of a model of economic growth, this implies that society's utility is driven not only by consumption possibilities but also by the state of natural assets.

[6] United States Department of Commerce (2010); New Zealand Ministry for the Environment (2010); UK Department for Business Enterprise and Regulatory Reform (2009); Eurostat Environmental Goods and Services Sector Data.

[7] For example Kennett and Steenblik (2005), New Zealand Ministry for the Environment (2010).

References

Eurostat Environmental Goods and Services Sector Data, available at http://epp.eurostat.ec.europa.eu/portal/page/portal/environmental_accounts/data/database.

Heal, G. M and B. Kriström (2005), "National Income and the Environment", in Karl-Göran Mäler and Jeffrey R. Vincent (eds.), *Handbook of Environmental Economics,* Elsevier, Amsterdam, pp. 1105-1618.

Hulten, C. R. and P. Schreyer (2010), "GDP, Technical Change, and the Measurement of Net Income: the Weitzman Model Revisited", *NBER Working Papers*, No. 16010, NBER, Massachusetts.

Kennett, M. and Steenblik, R. (2005), "Environmental Goods and Services: A Synthesis of Country Studies", *OECD Trade and Environment Working Papers,* No. 2005-03, OECD, Paris.

Nardo, M., M. Saisana, A. Saltelli, S. Tarantola, A. Hoffman and E. Giovannini (2005), "Handbook on Constructing Composite Indicators: Methodology and User Guide", *OECD Statistics Working Papers*, No. 2005/3, OECD, Paris.

New Zealand Ministry of the Environment (2010), *Green Economy: Facts and Figures for New Zealand*, New Zealand Ministry for the Environment, Wellington.

Nordhaus, W. (1995), "How Should We Measure Sustainable Income?", *Cowles Foundation Discussion Papers* 1101, Cowles Foundation for Research in Economics, Connecticut.

OECD (2011), Entrepreneurship at a Glance 2010, (forthcoming).

UNECE, OECD, Eurostat (2009), *Measuring Sustainable Development*, available at www.unece.org/stats/archive/03.03f.e.htm.

United Kingdom Department for Business Enterprise and Regulatory Reform (2009), "Low Carbon and Environmental Goods and Services: an Industry Analysis", study commissioned by the Department, UK Department for Business Enterprise and Regulatory Reform , London, available at www.berr.gov.uk/files/file50253.pdf.

United States Department of Commerce (2010), *Measuring the Green Economy*, United States Department of Commerce, Washington DC.

Weitzman, M. L. (1997), "Sustainability and Technological Progress", *Scandinavian Journal of Economics*, Vol. 99, Wiley-Blackwell, New Jersey, pp. 1-13.

Chapter 5. Delivering on green growth

Green growth should be conceived as a strategic complement to existing environmental and economic policy reform priorities. If governments wish to green the growth paths of their economies, they need to treat the policy challenges as being ones that go to the core of their economic strategies. This implies a leading role for finance, economy and environment agencies.

Strategies for green growth need a long-term vision incorporating:

- *Diagnosis of key constraints limiting returns to green investment and innovation.*

- *An assessment of environmental conditions and risks going forward.*

- *Links to structural economic reform priorities.*

- *Stakeholder engagement and cost-benefit analysis.*

- *Regular review of policies and measurement of progress.*

To support green growth strategies, the OECD will work in conjunction with countries, other international organisations and interested parties to further develop:

- *A comprehensive measurement framework and appropriate green growth indicators.*

- *Analytical tools for evaluating the relative effectiveness of green growth policies.*

- *Country and sector specific recommendations based on ongoing policy surveillance.*

Green growth encompasses a vast number of policy measures *e.g.* fiscal reform; regulatory policy reform; changes to education, research and innovation policies; jobs strategies; climate change mitigation instruments; energy efficiency measures; competition policy in network industries. Bringing together all these elements into a cogent framework is a challenge.

Green growth should be conceived as a strategic complement to existing priorities and areas for environmental and economic policy reform. Green growth strategies should target areas where there is clear beneficial overlap between environmental and economic policy and focus on finding cost-effective ways of attenuating environmental pressures, to begin the transition towards new patterns of growth that will avoid crossing critical environmental thresholds.

This chapter describes a process for constructing green growth strategies through prioritisation of policy reform. It also proposes a future work programme based on cross-country comparisons and benchmarking to further efforts to understand the effectiveness of policies aimed at raising living standards while accounting for the environmental risks that can undermine them.

Constructing green growth strategies

Green growth strategies should establish environmental priorities, diagnose key market constraints to delivering improvements, and match these with structural economic reform priorities.[1]

At the core of green growth are constraints or distortions in the economy which inhibit returns to "green" investment and innovation, *i.e.* activities which can foster economic growth and development while ensuring that natural assets continue to provide the resources and ecosystem services on which our well-being relies. Green growth strategies should focus on the most binding constraints, identifying major environmental priorities, and investigating any overlap between structural economic reform priorities and major constraints to green growth.

Constraints to green growth

Conceptually, three kinds of constraint to green growth might be addressed: government failures; market failures; and market imperfections. Government failures include policies like fossil fuel subsidies which reduce overall economic activity and result in environmental damage. Market failures, often associated with public goods like air quality or common pool resources like fisheries, include excess pollution due to environmental externalities or barriers to improved energy efficiency arising due to split incentives. Market imperfections are features of markets that can have problematic effects from the point of view of social welfare but for which there is no easy solution from a policy perspective *i.e.* these are inherent imperfections like economies of scale or natural monopoly characteristics in network industries which are not necessarily resolved by government intervention.

The resolution of government failures should be the top priority as these failures work against the cost effectiveness of other reforms and are more cost-effective to resolve than other kinds of failures. It would not, for example, be cost effective to introduce policy to control nutrient run-off on farms while fertiliser is being subsidised. Market failures should also be accorded high priority as there is a clear rationale for policy action and, in general, clear cost-effective policy options for dealing with them.

While these failures and imperfections represent fundamental constraints, in practice they overlap and do not necessarily map well to different economic circumstances and so do not provide a very rich way to think about constraints on green growth.

An alternative schematic, presented in Figure 5.1, divides low returns to "green" investment and innovation into two aspects. The first is low overall economic returns. This encompasses factors which create inertia in economic systems (*i.e.* fundamental barriers to change and innovation) and capacity constraints, or "low social returns".

Low economic returns to new activities can be a function of inertia in economic, human and physical systems. This inertia constrains the expansion of new or innovative production techniques, technologies and patterns of consumption. Constraints to green innovation are a mixture of market failure and market imperfection. Low returns to R&D are a market failure. Network effects (*e.g.* barriers to entry that arise from increasing returns to scale in networks) and the bias in the market towards existing technologies are examples of market imperfection. The exception to this is that government failure can arise from attempts to deal with these market failures (*e.g.* regulatory barriers to competition and government monopolies in network industries).

"Low social returns" implies the absence of enabling conditions for increasing returns to low environmental impact activities. These constraints reduce the choices of consumers and producers to pursue low impact activities. For example, inadequate electricity or water sanitation infrastructure may leads to water pollution or the use of high emission fuels or inefficient production of electricity. They can also include insufficient human capital such that people are not aware of alternative sources of energy or there is insufficient technical know-how to deploy them. In addition, at low levels of development a mixture of poor infrastructure with low human capital and institutional quality can mean heavy reliance on natural resource extraction and little incentive for improved natural resource use like sustainable forest management. These constraints reflect a mixture of government failure, market failures and market imperfections.

The second is low appropriability of returns. This is where market and government failures prevent people from capturing the full value of improved environmental outcomes and efficiency of resource use. Examples of market failure include a lack of incentives for energy efficient buildings (split incentives) or excessive agricultural water use and pollution or road transport emissions (*i.e.* negative externalities) which reduce local air quality. This also encompasses a lack of incentives to provide new or cheaper ways of doing things which can improve returns to "green" activities such as low emission energy sources or crop strains which lower the need for fertiliser use.

There are, however, some overlaps between market and government failures. For example, incomplete property rights are in many cases a market failure but they are listed as a government failure to reflect the inefficacy or absence of policy to address these well-known failures in cases such as over-fishing. Similarly, the presence of regulatory uncertainty is a major impediment to private actions to reduce greenhouse gas emissions even though excessive greenhouse gas emissions are essentially a result of market failure.

Figure 5.1.   Green growth diagnostic

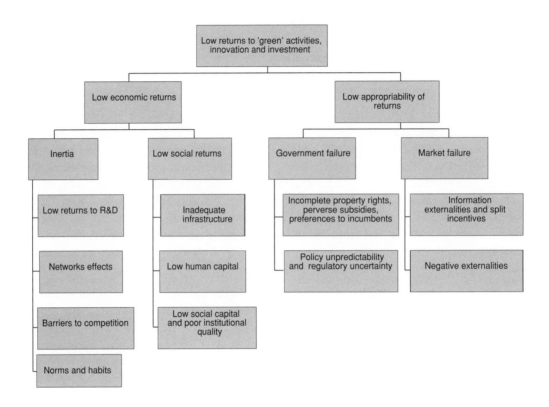

Source: OECD, concept based on Hausmann, Velasco and Rodrik (2008), "Growth Diagnostics" in J. Stiglitz and N. Serra, (eds), *The Washington Consensus Reconsidered: Towards a New Global Governance.*

The importance of constraints to green growth will vary according to level of development, economic context, and existing economic and environmental policy settings. Low human capital or inadequate infrastructure will tend to be associated with lower levels of economic development. Rectifying these constraints will be of high priority and perhaps a precondition to resolving many other constraints.

Where human capital is relatively abundant and infrastructure relatively well-supplied, the focus should first be on resolving government and market failures. In some countries and on some issues policy is already relatively advanced in this regard (such as in the case of fuel taxes in much of Europe). In these cases attention should turn to the inherent disadvantages that new technologies have relative to the installed capital base and policies that can help advance these.[2] Sequencing is important to the extent resolving low returns to activities with low environmental impact will create market conditions that are conducive to the introduction of new green technologies.

Identifying which constraints are most important is not, however, entirely sequential. In particular, while institutions in some countries may not presently be equipped to address some environmental externalities, government failures or split incentives may be able to be addressed. In other cases, environmental externalities may not be fully addressed but there may still be scope to address low returns to R&D.

One constraint which is likely to be common to all countries, regardless of development, is regulatory certainty *i.e.* the extent to which governments articulate and ideally legislate a clear plan for closing the gaps between private and social return so that people can plan and act without too much risk that governments will change the rules of the game.

Establishing environmental priorities

The relative importance of constraints to green growth will vary depending on environmental priorities. Table 5.1 maps constraints to green growth by key environmental challenges as discussed earlier.

Table 5.1.   Constraints on green growth by environmental challenges

Climate change	Health impacts of pollution
• Inadequate infrastructure • Low human and social capital • Incomplete property rights • Subsidies and preferences to incumbents • Negative externalities • Low returns to R&D • Network effects • Barriers to competition • Norms and habits • Information externalities and split incentives	• Inadequate infrastructure • Low human and social capital • Subsidies and preferences to incumbents • Negative externalities • Low returns to R&D • Barriers to competition • Norms and habits

Biodiversity loss	Water scarcity
• Low human and social capital • Incomplete property rights • Subsidies and preferences to incumbents • Negative externalities	• Inadequate infrastructure • Low human and social capital • Incomplete property rights • Subsidies and preferences to incumbents • Network effects

Environmental country-level priorities will be dictated to some extent by regional variation in terms of local environmental challenges alongside global environmental priorities, resource endowments and income levels. As a guide, these priorities should account for:

- *Certainty of impact*. As many environmental impacts are uncertain, the degree of evidence and probability of damages should be taken into account. Other things being equal, the more certain the impact, the more importance it should be given in the design of policy. One exception may be climate change because of the risk of non-linear catastrophic change.

- *Potential for non-linear change*. The greater the likelihood of non-linear, abrupt or catastrophic change, the higher the priority.

- *Timing*. When are impacts likely to become severe or critical? The connection between actions now and longer term damage should be taken into account *i.e.* potential path dependency and the risk of irreversibility.

- *Severity of impact.* How large, in absolute terms, could the costs be? Where there are threats of serious or catastrophic damage it is not appropriate to use the lack of full scientific certainty as a reason for postponing cost-effective measures to prevent or minimise this damage.

- *Distribution of impact.* If environmental impacts are concentrated in a particular sector of the economy, how important is that sector in terms of economic size, for low income groups or cultural or other values what is its potential to affect other sectors of the economy. More generally, would the environmental impacts affect vulnerable groups disproportionately?

The formulation of strategies should follow a well-defined and iterative process:

- Objectives should be informed by an assessment of business as usual (BAU) projections with respect to economic and environmental trends (taking into account population and economic growth).

- Assessment of BAU should form the basis for developing a long-term vision, with high-level buy-in and through dialogue with major stakeholders within and outside government.

- The establishment of a long term vision should also be informed by robust cost-benefit analysis.

- Given a set of objectives, the policy process should proceed to identify least-cost policy options and areas for intervention - to identify policy priorities and sequencing. Policy should be robust but flexible, with capacity for adaptation as new information becomes available.

- Implementation of policies should incorporate regular monitoring and review of the effects of policy and procedures for adapting policy settings.

The diagnosis of key constraints will require country-specific information and data from across the environment and the economy as well as an appreciation for links to global economic and environmental trends. The indicators discussed in Chapter 4 of this report provide high-level measures which can be used to inform a diagnosis of constraints to green growth.

Links to structural economic reform priorities

Ranking of reform efforts should also take account of the links between conventional structural economic reform and potential key constraints to green growth (Table 5.2). Priority should be given to cases where constraints on green growth translate equally into constraints on growth more generally. This might include improving infrastructure or increasing innovation incentives. Indeed, many of the constraints identified in Figure 5.1 might equally feature on a structural reform agenda.

In other cases there will be apparent trade-offs between strengthening the market economy and pursuing green growth. However, these should be scrutinised for false trade-offs where reducing constraints to green growth might result in higher well-being not reflected in structural reform priorities. This would be the case in targeting many environmental externalities.

There will also be cases where green growth priorities conflict with structural reform priorities because of the need to take a precautionary stance to deal with systemic environmental risks. This is most likely to occur where the major constraints to green growth are related to path dependency, such as subsidising new network infrastructure or incentivising deployment of renewable energy. These sorts of actions carry both a high risk of policy failure and a potentially high pay-off in terms of reducing systemic environmental risk. In this regard the apparent conflict between structural reform and green growth priorities is an indication of the need for caution and perhaps the need to explore whether resolution of other constraints should not be afforded higher priority.

Table 5.2. Constraints on green growth and structural economic reform priorities

Inadequate infrastructure

- Improve the quality of infrastructure
- Strengthen competition in network industries

Low human and social capital and institutional quality

- Strengthen the legal system
- Improve educational efficiency/outcomes
- Improve incentives for formal labour market participation

Incomplete property rights, subsidies, preferences to incumbents

- Reduce barriers to foreign ownership/investment/trade
- Reduce regulatory barriers to competition
- Reform/simplify product market regulations
- Phase out environmentally harmful energy subsidies
- Reform/strengthen the structure of the tax system

Negative externalities

- Reform/strengthen the structure of the tax system
- Reduce barriers to foreign ownership/investment/trade

Low returns to R&D

- Strengthen R&D and innovation incentives
- Improve intellectual property rights regime

Network effects

- Strengthen competition in network industries

Barriers to competition

- Reform/simplify product market regulations
- Reduce regulatory barriers to competition

Green Growth Strategy: Next steps

The delivery of the *Towards Green Growth* and *Towards Green Growth – Monitoring Progress: OECD Indicators* reports at the 2011 Ministerial Council Meeting (MCM) will mark the starting point of the OECD longer-term agenda to support national and international efforts to achieve green growth. Building on the Organisation-wide work underpinning these two reports, green growth would be further mainstreamed in OECD policy surveillance to provide continued guidance on a number of country-, sector- and issue-specific areas. Table 5.3 provides an indicative overview of potential directions for future work.

Table 5.3.   Examples of OECD work on green growth, 2011-12

Timeline	Deliverables
2011 MCM	• Towards Green Growth – Green Growth Strategy synthesis report • Towards Green Growth - Monitoring Progress: OECD Indicators

Post 2011 MCM	• A Green Growth Strategy for Food and Agriculture: Preliminary Report
	• Joint IEA/OECD Green Growth Study for Energy
	• Green growth monitoring work:
	    o Green growth indicators
	    o Further green growth chapters in Economic Surveys and Environmental Performance Reviews
	    o Green growth reports for emerging economies
	    o Monitoring green investment protectionism concerns
	• Report on green growth and developing countries
	• Report on green innovation
	• Green growth and biodiversity
	• Green growth and water
	• Green Cities Programme
	• Renewable energy and rural development
	• Project on green financing
	• Environmental regulations and growth
	• Green fiscal revenue
	• Job potential of a shift towards a low-carbon economy
	• Report on the local transition to a green economy

Towards cross-country comparison and policy evaluation

To support green growth strategies, the OECD should continue to further develop and determine a suite of appropriate green growth indicators that could be used to evaluate the relative effectiveness of green growth policies in the future.

A diagnostic exercise could build on the methodology used by the OECD in its flagship publication *Going for Growth* for evaluating economic performance and structural economic policy settings in OECD countries and major emerging economies. The *Going for Growth* methodology combines indicators of countries' economic performance and indicators of policy settings with empirical evidence on the links between the two and country-specific expertise. Three reform priorities are identified based on areas where indicators show that both economic performance and policy settings are weak relative to other countries. A further two reform priorities are chosen based solely on country-specific expertise and analysis. Steps taken to address these priorities are evaluated annually and priorities are updated every two years.

A first step would start with monitoring environmental performance. Chapter 4 highlights some of the issues and indicators that might be used (Table 4.1). For instance, these might include changes in: CO_2 emissions intensity; nutrient intensity; intensity of water use; and air pollution.[3] Candidate environmental priorities would be established based on relative performance in these different areas compared to other countries (*e.g.* the average).[4]

Indicators of environmental policy settings would then be compared against environmental and economic performance to identify candidate priorities for policy improvement. Relatively weak policy which overlapped with poor environmental performance would indicate a candidate reform priority. Relatively heavy reliance on inflexible policy instruments which coincided with relatively poor economic performance would imply growth improvements from altering the composition of environmental policy and thus suggest another candidate priority.

Indicators of environmental policy settings will have to be further developed for this task. Discussion in this Report has been focussed on understanding the cost effectiveness of environmental policy instruments and their relationship with economic policies for which we have evidence of links to growth. Indicators of environmental policy settings should be developed in ways that enable policy analysis to go beyond this and to provide a more complete assessment of the way that policy affects both economic and environmental performance.[5]

Candidate environmental policy reforms would then be linked to *Going for Growth* by considering potential synergies with candidate economic policy reforms *e.g.* over-reliance on direct taxes intersecting with the need for price instruments to deal with local air pollution.[6] The resulting economic and environmental policy priorities would collectively constitute green growth reform priorities.

As is the case of *Going for Growth*, there would need to be some green growth priorities which are established through country-specific analysis. Indicator-based priorities would also need to account for country-specific economic and environmental circumstances. The diagnostic framework described above would be useful in this regard.

Ultimately, the objective would be to institute a mainstreamed process of policy monitoring and evaluation. This kind of project would, over time, become a tool to increase collective knowledge about how policies contribute to green growth. It would be a way for countries to measure their own progress relative to others and learn from the experience of others. Most importantly it would be a step towards reframing growth in a way which better accounts for natural assets and for the environmental risks that could ultimately undermine economic growth and development.

Notes

[1] In this discussion we draw on structural economic reform priorities from the OECD's *Going for Growth* work. This is by way of example. Other economic reform priorities could be considered in the application of this framework.

[2] The nature of this disadvantage will vary according to existing regulatory environments. In some cases, the regulatory environment will be such that incumbent firms enjoy an advantage over new entrants. In other cases the lack of a supporting network may prevent deployment of innovative technologies.

[3] Existing measures may need to be adapted for use in cross-country analysis to account for underlying rates of change in the composition of economic activity; in much the same way that economic performance measures are decomposed to take into account different drivers of economic performance.

[4] This would also need to be supplemented by considerations of the absolute levels of environmental performance and the extent to which an economy is decoupling environmental impacts from growth in absolute or relative terms.

[5] To do this, policy indicators will need to reflect both the degree of stringency of policies (*e.g.* effective price of carbon), the design of policies (*e.g.* flexibility) and anticipated environmental outcomes.

[6] These priorities would not necessarily need to be the ones finally identified for *Going for Growth*.

References

Hausmann, R., A. Velasco and D. Rodrik (2008), "Growth Diagnostics" in J. Stiglitz and N. Serra (eds.), *The Washington Consensus Reconsidered: Towards a New Global Governance*, Oxford University Press, New York.

Further reading

Dellink, R., G. Briner and C. Clapp (2010), "Costs, Revenues, and Effectiveness of the Copenhagen Accord Emission Pledges for 2020", *OECD Environment Working Papers*, No. 22, OECD, Paris.

Deschenes, O. (2010), "Climate Policy and Labor Markets", *NBER Working Papers,* No. 16111, National Bureau of Economic Research, Cambridge, Massachusetts.

Duval, R. (2008), "A Taxonomy of Instruments to Reduce Greenhouse Gas Emissions and their Interactions", *OECD Economics Department Working Papers*, No. 636, OECD, Paris.

EC (European Commission) (2009), *Employment in Europe 2009*, European Commission, Brussels.

Edler, J. and L. Georghiou (2007), "Public Procurement and Innovation: Resurrecting the Demand Side", *Research Policy*, Elsevier, Amsterdam, Vol. 36, pp. 949-963.

European Commission (2010), iGrow Green: Setting up an Indicator-Based Assessment Framework to Identify Country-Specific Challenges to Promote a More Resource Efficient Europe (Draft paper unpublished).

FAO (2009), "How to feed the World in 2050", Issue Brief from the How to Feed the World 2050 High-Level Expert Forum, Rome, 12-14 October available at www.fao.org/fileadmin/templates/wsfs/docs/expert_paper/How_to_Feed_the_World_in_2050.pdf.

Fischer, A., L. Petersen, C. Feldkötter and W. Huppert (2007), "Sustainable Governance of Natural Resources and Institutional Change – an Analytical Framework", *Public Administration and Development,* Vol. 27, John Wiley & Sons, Ltd., Massachusetts, pp. 123-137.

Fullerton, D., A. Leicester and S. Smith (2010), "Environmental Taxes", Chapter 5 in *The Mirrlees Review – Reforming the Tax System for the 21st Century*, Institute for Fiscal Studies, London,available at www.ifs.org.uk/mirrleesReview.

Ghosh, S. and R. Nanda (2010), "Venture Capital Investment in the Clean Energy Sector", *Harvard Business School Working Papers,* No. 11-020, Harvard Business School, Massachusetts.

Grazi, F., J. van den Bergh and J. van Ommeren (2008), "An Empirical Analysis of Urban Form, Transport, and Global Warming", *The Energy Journal*, Vol. 29, No. 4, IAEE (International Research Centre on Environment and Development), Paris, pp. 97-122.

Heal, G. (2000), Nature and the Market Place: Capturing the Value of Ecosystem Services, Island Press, Washington DC.

Hoekman, B. M., K. E. Maskus, K. Saggi (2005), "Transfer of Technology to Developing Countries: Unilateral and Multilateral Policy Options", *World Development*, Vol. 33, No. 10, Elsevier, Montreal, pp. 1587-1602.

Inderst, G. (2009), "Pension Fund Investment in Infrastructure", *OECD Working Papers on Insurance and Private Pensions*, No. 32, available at www.oecd.org/dataoecd/41/9/42052208.pdf.

ITF (2011), "Green Growth for Transport", *Discussion Paper*, No. 2011-02, ITF, OECD, Paris, summary available at www.internationaltransportforum.org/jtrc/DiscussionPapers/DP201102.pdf.

Jackson, T. (2009), *Prosperity Without Growth?: Economics for a Finite Planet,* Report of the Sustainable Development Commission, Earthscan Limited, Oxford.

Jaffe, A. B., S. R. Peterson, P. R. Portney and R. N. Stavins (1995), "Environmental Regulation and the Competitiveness of U.S. Manufacturing: What Does the Evidence Tell Us?", *Journal of Economic Literature*, Vol. 33, No. 1, American Economic Association Publications, Pittsburgh, pp. 132-163.

Johnstone, N., I. Haščič and M. Kalamova (2010), "Environmental Policy Design Characteristics and Technological Innovation: Evidence from Patent Data", *OECD Environment Working Papers,* No. 16, OECD, Paris.

Jones, C. and P. Romer (2009), "The New Kaldor Facts: Ideas, Institutions, Population, and Human Capital", *NBER Working Papers*, No.15094, NBER, Cambridge, Massachusetts.

Kalamova, M., C. Kaminker and N. Johnstone (2011), "Sources of Finance, Investment Policies and Plant Entry in the Renewable Energy Sector", OECD, Paris (forthcoming).

Keller, W. (1996), "Absorptive Capacity: On the Creation and Acquisition of Technology in Development", *Journal of Development Economics,* Vol. 49, Elsevier, Amsterdam, pp. 199–227.

Llamas, M. R. (2003), "Lessons Learnt from the Impact of the Neglected Role of Groundwater in Spain's Water Policy", in A.S. Alsharhan and W.W. Wood (eds.), *Water Resources Perspectives: Evaluation, Management and Policy*, Elsevier, Amsterdam.

Mancusi, M. (2008), "International Spillovers and Absorptive Capacity: A Cross-Country Cross-Sector Analysis based on Patents and Citations", *Journal of International Economics,* Vol. 76, No. 2, pp. 155-165.

Maskus, K. E. (2000), *Intellectual Property Rights in the Global Economy,* Institute for International Economics, Washington DC.

Metcalf, G. E. (2009), "Tax Policies for Low-Carbon Technologies," *NBER Working Papers,* No. 15054, NBER, Cambridge, Massachusetts, available at www.nber.org/papers/w15054.pdf.

Metz, B., O. R. Davidson, J. Martens, S. N. M. van Rooijen and L. van Wie McGrory (eds.) (2000), "Methodological and Technological Issues in Technology Transfer", *IPCC Special Reports on Climate Change,* Cambridge University Press, New York.

Millennium Ecosystem Assessment (2005), *Ecosystems and Human Well-Being: General Synthesis,* Island Press, Washington DC, available at www.maweb.org/en/Synthesis.aspx.

Myers, N. and J. L. Simon (1994), *Scarcity or Abundance? A Debate on the Environment*, W. W. Norton & Co Inc Publishing, New York.

Ockwell, D., J. Watson, A. Mallett, R. Haum, G. MacKerron and A. Verbeken (2010), "Enhancing Developing Country Access to Eco-Innovation: The Case of Technology Transfer and Climate Change in a Post-2012 Policy Framework", *OECD Environment Working Papers*, No. 12, OECD, Paris.

Ockwell, D., J. Watson, G. MacKerron, P. Pal and F. Yamin (2008), "Key Policy Considerations for Facilitating Low Carbon Technology Transfer to Developing Countries", *Energy Policy* Vol. 36, No. 11, Elsevier, Amsterdam, pp. 4104-4115.

OECD (2001), Environmentally Related Taxes in OECD Countries: Issues and Strategies, OECD, Paris.

OECD (2002), Foreign Direct Investment and the Environment: Lessons from the Mining Sector, OECD Global Forum on International Investment, OECD, Paris.

OECD (2003), The Environmental Performance of Public Procurement, OECD, Paris.

OECD (2008), Environmental Performance of Agriculture in OECD Countries Since 1990, OECD, Paris.

OECD (2008), Environmental Policy, Technological Innovation and Patents, OECD, Paris.

OECD (2008), More than Just Jobs: Workforce Development in a Skills-Based Economy, OECD, Paris.

OECD (2009), Econometric Analysis of the Impacts of the UK Climate Change Levy and Climate Change Agreements on Firms' Fuel Use and Innovation Activity, OECD, Paris.

OECD (2009), Environmental Cross-Compliance in Agriculture, OECD, Paris.

OECD (2009), OECD Science, Technology and Industry Scoreboard 2009, OECD, Paris.

OECD (2009), The Political Economy of Reform: Lessons from Pensions, Product Markets and Labour Markets in Ten OECD Countries, OECD, Paris.

OECD (2010), "Greener and Smarter - ICTs, the Environment and Climate Change", OECD, Paris, available at www.oecd.org/dataoecd/27/12/45983022.pdf.

OECD (2010), Economic Policy Reforms 2010: Going for Growth, OECD, Paris.

OECD (2010), Going for Growth database, OECD, Paris, available at http://stats.oecd.org/Index.aspx?DataSetCode=GROWTH.

OECD (2010), Pricing Water Resources and Water and Sanitation Services, OECD, Paris.

OECD (2011), "Climate Change Mitigation Policies and Employment" (forthcoming).

OECD (2011), "Green Growth and Biodiversity" (forthcoming).

OECD (2011), "Pro-Active Policies for Green Growth and the Market Economy", OECD Competition Committee Roundtable (forthcoming).

OECD (2011), Better Policies to Support Eco-Innovation, OECD, Paris.

OECD (2011), Towards Green Growth - Monitoring Progress: OECD Indicators.

OECD (2011j), Tools for Delivering on Green Growth, OECD, Paris, available at www.oecd.org/greengrowth.

OECD, Wikiprogress, OECD's Work on Measuring Progress, OECD, Paris, available at www.wikiprogress.org/index.php/Main_Page.

Ouellette, L.L. (2010), "Addressing the Green Patent Global Deadlock Through Bayl-Dole Reform", Yale Law Journal, Vol. 119, The Yale Law Journal Company, Inc., Connecticut, pp. 1727-1738.

Paroussos, L. and P. Capros (2009), "Assessment of the Employment Effects from i) an Increase in Energy Efficiency, and ii) a Rise in Renewable Sectors", Research Report for the European Commission, Brussels.

Pearce, D., G. Atkinson and S. Mourato (2006), Cost-Benefit Analysis and the Environment, OECD, Paris.

Philibert, C. and J. Pershing (2002), Beyond Kyoto: Energy Dynamics and Climate Stabilisation, OECD/IEA, Paris.

Pichert, D. and K. Katsikopoulos (2008), "Green Defaults: Information Presentation and Pro Environmental Behaviour", *Journal of Economic Psychology,* Vol. 28, Elsevier, Amsterdam, pp. 63-73.

Prakash, A. and M. Potoski (2006), The Voluntary Environmentalists: Green Clubs, ISO 14001, and Voluntary Environmental Regulations, Cambridge University Press, Cambridge.

Prud'homme, R. (2010), "Electric Vehicles: A Tentative Economic and Environmental Evaluation", paper presented at 2010 ITF-KOTI Joint Seminar on Green Growth in Transport, 25 November 2010, International Transport Forum, Paris, available at www.internationaltransportforum.org/Proceedings/GreenGrowth2010/Prudhomme.pdf.

Shah, T., J. Burke and K. Villholth (2007), "Groundwater: A Global Assessment of Scale and Significance" in International Water Management Institute (ed.), *Water for Food, Water for Life: A Comprehensive Assessment of Water Management*, Earthscan, London.

Smil, V. (2003), The Earth's Biosphere: Evolution, Dynamics, and Change, MIT, Massachusetts.

Steenblik, R. (2010), "Subsidies in the Traditional Energy Sector", in Joost Pauwelyn (ed.), *Global Challenges at the Intersection of Trade, Energy and the Environment*, Centre for Trade and Economic Integration, Geneva, pp. 183-192.

Sutinen, J. G. (2008), "Major Challenges for Fishery Policy Reform: A Political Economy Perspective", *OECD Food, Agriculture and Fisheries Working Papers*, No. 8, OECD, Paris.

UN, EC, IMF, World Bank, OECD (2003), *Integrated Environmental and Economic Accounting (SEEA2003), UN Statistical Division*, New York, available at http://unstats.un.org/UNSD/envAccounting/seea2003.pdf.

UNDP, UNEP, World Bank and World Resources Institute (2008), *World Resources 2008: Roots of Resilience - Growing the Wealth of the Poor,* Washington DC.

World Bank (2004), *Sustaining Forests: A Development Strategy*, The World Bank, Washington DC.

World Bank, World Bank World Development Indicators, Washington DC available at http://data.worldbank.org/indicator.

Worrell, E., M.D. Levine, L.K. Price, N.C. Martin, R. van den Broek and K. Blok (1997), *Potentials and Policy Implications of Energy and Material Efficiency Improvement*, United Nations Division for Sustainable Development, New York.

Xepapadeas, A. (2005), "Economic Growth and the Environment", Chapter 23, *Handbook of Environmental Economics*, Vol. 3, Elsevier B.V., Amsterdam.

Zarksy, L. and K. Gallagher (2003), "Searching for the Holy Grail? Making FDI work for Sustainable Development", *Analytical Paper,* World Wide Fund for Nature, Geneva, available at http://ase.tufts.edu/gdae/publications/articles_reports/KG-LZ_FDI_report.pdf.

Annex 1.   Harnessing freedom of investment for green growth

Communication by the Freedom of Investment Roundtable

International investment is a vital source of finance and a powerful vector of innovation and technology transfer as countries address the effects of climate change and seek to promote green growth. Recognising this and desiring to make a contribution to the development of green growth policies, the Freedom of Investment (FOI) Roundtable hosted by the OECD has discussed important aspects of the role of international investment in supporting the realisation of countries' green growth objectives.[1]

The FOI Roundtable has explored in particular the issue of green investment protectionism and the interaction of international environmental and investment law. It also appreciates that greening the economy can be an important source of growth, as emphasised by work of the OECD Investment Committee and the OECD Environmental Policy Committee on enhancing business' contribution to greening the economy and unlocking green foreign direct investment (FDI).[2]

This document sets forth findings by FOI Delegates[3] on the role of international investment in supporting the realisation of countries' green growth objectives; specifically it underlines the importance of (i) mutual supportiveness of international environmental and investment law; (ii) monitoring investment treaty practices regarding the environment; (iii) ensuring the integrity and competence, and improving the transparency of investor-state dispute settlement; (iv) strengthening compliance with international investment law through prior review of proposed environmental measures and through effective environmental law and regulatory practices; (v) vigilance against green protectionism; (vi) encouraging business contribution to greening the economy; and (vii) spurring green growth through FDI.

A draft version of these findings was circulated for comment to experts, international organisations, civil society representatives and FOI participants. The Roundtable expresses its appreciation for the comments received, which have been carefully considered. The findings reflect extensive analysis and discussion in the Roundtable.

Mutual supportiveness of international environmental and investment law

The international investment policy community has a strong interest in effective policy frameworks that clarify environmental responsibilities and sharpen incentives for governments and businesses to live up to these responsibilities. Effective international environmental law and standards allow the international investment policy community to pursue with greater confidence its agenda of investment liberalisation, promotion and protection, in support of sustainable development. Important international environmental standards for investors can be found in international instruments such as the OECD Guidelines for Multinational Enterprises and the United Nations *Global Compact*.

> *FOI Delegates believe that their governments' environmental and investment policy goals are compatible. They also consider that those goals can be made mutually reinforcing and that this mutual supportiveness should be fostered.*

Monitoring investment treaty practices regarding the environment

A stocktaking exercise has shown that specific references to the environment are included in a limited number of investment agreements. However, the number is increasing. Governments participating in FOI Roundtables that have been respondents in investor-state cases challenging public policy measures now tend more explicitly to address such public policy issues, including environmental issues, on a systematic basis in investment treaties.

> *FOI Delegates consider that governments should continue to monitor their investment treaty practices with regard to environmental goals.*

Investor-state dispute settlement and the environment

The investor-state dispute settlement (ISDS) system may impose substantial liability on governments where public measures are found to be inconsistent with their international investment law obligations. It is essential to ensure the integrity and competence of investor-state arbitration tribunals. Transparency and openness of ISDS enhances its legitimacy by ensuring that the public is aware of the claims made, how the State is responding, and the tribunal's decisions. Governments, investors, academics and others can analyse the processes and outcomes. Since 2005 when the OECD Investment Committee adopted a Statement supporting greater transparency in ISDS, there has been progress in improving transparency. Still, investor-state cases can remain unknown to the public under many investment treaties. Ongoing negotiations at UNCITRAL to develop a legal standard on transparency for treaty-based investor-state arbitration and the expanded use of transparency provisions in investment treaties should assist further in advancing the goals of the 2005 Statement, including in environment-related cases.

> *FOI Delegates consider that governments should seek to ensure that investor-state arbitrations, including in cases involving environmental matters, are conducted in a transparent manner including the possibility for open hearings and, where appropriate, third-party participation.*

Preventing conflicts

It is important that new environmental measures generally respect key investment law disciplines such as non-discrimination, creating a level playing field for all investors. This process is most effective and efficient if it is integrated into policy design at an early stage: policies can be better-designed and expensive conflicts are avoided.

Good practices for regulation and governance in the environmental area are also of fundamental importance for preventing conflicts. Environmental impact assessments of significant new investments are important to identify and prevent conflicts between economic development and the environment.

> *FOI Delegates consider that governments should review their new proposed environmental measures for compliance with investment law obligations, such as those regarding non-discrimination.*

Vigilance against green protectionism

Some countries have expressed concern that the green growth policy agenda could be captured by protectionist interests. However, OECD policy monitoring suggests that to date investment protectionism associated with green growth policies is not a major problem. None of the 42 countries that report regularly to the OECD about investment measures have reported measures involving overt discrimination against non-resident or foreign investors in relation to environmental policy. Neither have participating countries reported to date serious concerns about such measures by other countries.

Nonetheless, vigilance is encouraged. Environmental policy measures that appear to be neutral may potentially involve *de facto* discrimination. In addition, some environment-related state aids (such as grants, loan guarantees or capital injections for individual firms), now widely used including as part of emergency investment measures in the wake of the financial crisis, may potentially pose risks to competition.

> *FOI Delegates consider that governments should ensure that measures taken to pursue green growth are consistent with their international obligations including their international investment law obligations. The monitoring of measures, including state aid, for protectionist intent or effects should continue, including as part of ongoing policy monitoring at the Freedom of Investment Roundtable and in the joint OECD-UNCTAD Reports on Investment Measures for the G-20.*

Encouraging business' contribution to greening the economy

Businesses have a key role to play in the transition to a green economy. More companies are responding to the challenges and opportunities of moving towards a low-carbon economy, developing environmentally-friendly products and services, and reporting on and reducing their greenhouse gas emissions. Stronger government policies are needed to encourage more companies to take such action and to encourage companies to go further and adopt more ambitious measures - reducing waste, adopting low-carbon technologies and shifting to renewable energies.

> *FOI Delegates consider that governments should establish or reinforce their policy framework to encourage, in a manner consistent with their international commitments, the positive contribution of business to green growth.*

Spurring green growth through FDI

FDI contributes to the production of environmental goods and services, and to transfers of technology, management processes and capital that can improve the environment. More such FDI will be required in the future. Investment law protections can play a very important role in encouraging the necessary investment.

Lack of comparable data between countries, however, obscures both FDI's contribution and the possible obstacles to it. A definition of FDI in support of green growth (or of key categories of such investment) would help governments use scarce public resources to lever private investment, assess policy performance in providing a positive framework for investment in support of green growth, and better identify and lower any hurdles to such investment.

> *FOI Delegates consider that governments should contribute to efforts to measure FDI in support of green growth and to assess policy performance in providing a framework to encourage it.*

Notes

[1] The OECD-hosted Freedom of Investment (FOI) Roundtable is an intergovernmental forum that brings together OECD member and non-member governments from around the globe at regular meetings. It helps governments design better policies to reconcile openness to international investment with legitimate regulation in the public interest.

[2] See www.oecd.org/daf/investment/cc.

[3] This document has been approved by delegates to the FOI Roundtable from the following governments: Australia, Austria, Belgium, Canada, Chile, the Czech Republic, Denmark, Estonia, Finland, France, Germany, Greece, Hungary, Iceland, Ireland, Israel, Italy, Japan, Korea, Luxembourg, Mexico, Morocco, the Netherlands, New Zealand, Norway, Peru, Poland, Portugal, the Slovak Republic, Slovenia, Spain, Sweden, Switzerland, Romania, Turkey, United Kingdom and the United States. Together with the delegate from the European Commission, who has also approved the document, these delegates are referred to herein as the "FOI Delegates".

ORGANISATION FOR ECONOMIC CO-OPERATION AND DEVELOPMENT

The OECD is a unique forum where governments work together to address the economic, social and environmental challenges of globalisation. The OECD is also at the forefront of efforts to understand and to help governments respond to new developments and concerns, such as corporate governance, the information economy and the challenges of an ageing population. The Organisation provides a setting where governments can compare policy experiences, seek answers to common problems, identify good practice and work to co-ordinate domestic and international policies.

The OECD member countries are: Australia, Austria, Belgium, Canada, Chile, the Czech Republic, Denmark, Estonia, Finland, France, Germany, Greece, Hungary, Iceland, Ireland, Israel, Italy, Japan, Korea, Luxembourg, Mexico, the Netherlands, New Zealand, Norway, Poland, Portugal, the Slovak Republic, Slovenia, Spain, Sweden, Switzerland, Turkey, the United Kingdom and the United States. The European Union takes part in the work of the OECD.

OECD Publishing disseminates widely the results of the Organisation's statistics gathering and research on economic, social and environmental issues, as well as the conventions, guidelines and standards agreed by its members.

OECD PUBLISHING, 2, rue André-Pascal, 75775 PARIS CEDEX 16
(97 2011 06 1 P) ISBN 978-92-64-09497-0 – No. 58169 2011-07